ANSEL ADAMS

THE EARLY YEARS

ANSEL ADAMS

THE EARLY YEARS

KAREN E. QUINN AND THEODORE E. STEBBINS, JR.

To Pene and Sherb
In celebration of our years together. Fondly, Saundy and Bill

MUSEUM OF FINE ARTS, BOSTON

Christmas 1991

Library of Congress Cat. card no. 91-50674
ISBN 0-87846-345-3

Tritone separations made by Richard M. A.. Benson
Designed by Carl Zahn
Printed by Franklin Graphics, Providence R. I.

Cover Photographs:
Front:
3. *Glacier Point*, 1927.
Back:
11. *Eagle Dance,* about 1928-9.

"Ansel Adams: The Early Years" was organized by the Museum of Fine Arts, Boston and was held from October 8 – December 29, 1991.

INTRODUCTION

The Museum of Fine Arts is pleased to present the third in a series of exhibitions devoted to the work of major American photographers of the twentieth century and drawn entirely from the unique resources of the William H. Lane Collection. Both of the earlier exhibitions — "Charles Sheeler: The Photographs" (1987), a survey of the whole photographic oeuvre of one of the key American modernists, and "Weston's Westons: Portraits and Nudes" (1989), a study of the figurative work of another giant of American art — consisted wholly of original prints that came to the Lane Collection from the estates of the two artists.

Now, with "Ansel Adams: The Early Years," we turn to perhaps the most familiar figure in the history of the medium. Ansel Adams's name is synonymous with landscape photography, particularly with the glories of Yosemite, the Sierra, and the Southwest. The present exhibition is devoted to Adams's early work, from *"Wind"* of 1919 and the rarely seen "Parmelian Prints" of 1927 to the work of 1930 — 1941, his first eleven years as a full-time, professional photographer. The richness of the Lane Collection makes it possible for us to include many unfamiliar images — some completely unknown — along with a selection of Adams's signature pictures. In the prints of the late 1920s, we can study the roots of his crystalline, romantic landscape style. And in comparing early and later prints of the same or related images — as we do with two versions of the famous *Monolith – The Face of Half Dome*, (pls. 6 and 7) — we discover the effects of changing time, scale, paper, and printing techniques on pictures we thought we knew. We see a photographer experimenting with a wide variety of subjects, of course making his archetypal views of Yosemite and the West, but also picturing people with great understanding, creating ironic images of outdoor sculpture and museum storerooms, making abstractions from wallpaper or an old piano, exploring both the sorrowful and joyous sides of nature. Adams's work of these years reminds us, too, of his modernist roots, as in different works one finds him paying homage to Stieglitz, Strand, or Weston.

The prints from which this exhibition was drawn were collected by the Lanes between 1967 and 1973. Adams collaborated with them, helping them to acquire a "well balanced and definitive cross-section"[1] of his work, and inscribing each one with title, date, and other pertinent information. Some of the prints in the Lane Collection are unique; *Mount Robson From Mount Resplendent* (cat. no. 10), for example, Adams inscribed "Valuable — only extant print." Many others are rare vintage prints, contemporary with the negatives; on these Adams wrote "original print." Others still were printed especially for the Lanes between 1967 and 1973. Thus, the first of the Shipwreck Series of 1932 (pl. 11), was marked as an original print, while the others in the series (cat. nos. 24-28) have the no-less-effective — but different — look of prints made forty years later. Ansel Adams not only helped the Lanes to create an unsurpassed collection of his own work, but he also played a key role in the formation of the Lane Collection as a whole. He and Lane began their thirty-year friendship in October, 1954, when Lane and their mutual friend Charles Sheeler came to San Francisco after attending the opening of Sheeler's important retrospective in Los Angeles.[2] On October 25, 1954, Adams initiated their extraordinary correspondence "reporting on that benign prophet you left in my care," (referring of course to Sheeler), and then characteristically recruiting Lane for Sierra Club membership. The following year Lane sought Adams's assistance in securing West Coast engagements for the great tenor Roland Hayes, who was then being managed by Lane; Adams helped, and shortly thereafter made a portrait of Hayes in California.

Lane started to collect photography in a dedicated way during the mid-1960s, beginning with his acquisition of Charles

Sheeler's photographic estate. By 1967 he had determined to gather truly definitive collections of the work of the two West Coast masters, Ansel Adams and Edward Weston — among others. Over the next several years, Ansel and Virginia Adams acted as generous hosts, guides, and collaborators in building the collection. Lane, for his part, was the model collector; he was the first person ever to approach Adams with the desire to form a broad, archival collection of his best work, and the first to study it with such intense concern for quality. The process of selecting the Adams prints went on for six years, with letters, long lists, and packages of prints criss-crossing the country, and throughout, the mutual spirit of friendship and cooperation was never strained. As Adams wrote Lane, "It was a GREAT DAY for photography when you came this way!!!"[3]

The Adams-Lane correspondence deals with a wide variety of matters — the planning of visits East and West, Adams's work as a consultant to the Polaroid Company, the work of Imogen Cunningham, Wynn Bullock, Brett Weston and especially Edward Weston (Ansel and Virginia had introduced the Lanes to Cole and Brett, thus smoothing the way for the Lanes' concurrent purchases of Edward's work from his sons). Ansel discusses his books and other projects, turns to Lane for financial and estate planning advice, and on one occasion sends him a Polaroid "MP-3" camera; he keeps him up to date on the prints he's making to fill his vast order, and on developments with the Friends of Photography. In a letter to Lane in January, 1976, Adams makes clear the extent to which he had entrusted to this collector some of his rarest and finest early work: Adams explained that a friend of his would like to see "some of my early prints and some of the more unusual images that you have," and concluded, "He would like to see some unpublished things, and I told him that your collection would be the place to look."[4]

Ansel Adams's last letter to the Lanes is dated July 15, 1983. The Lanes had sent a copy of the catalogue, *The Lane Collection: 20th Century Paintings in the American Tradition* (1983), and Adams responded by commenting: "The selection of paintings reminds me of a conclave of old friends. You have certainly built a remarkable collection of works of art! I hope someday the world can see your photography collection."[5]

We are proud indeed to be bringing to the world this magnificent collection of American art.

THEODORE E. STEBBINS, JR.
John Moors Cabot Curator of American Paintings

Notes:

1. Letter Agreement between William H. Lane and Ansel Adams, October 28, 1967 (Lane Collection).

2. Charles Sheeler: A Retrospective Exhibition, organized by Frederick Wight at UCLA, opened in Los Angeles October 11, 1954.

3. Letter, Ansel Adams to William H. Lane, September 1, 1967 (Lane Collection).

4. Letter, Ansel Adams to William H. Lane, January 17, 1976 (Lane Collection).

5. Letter, Ansel Adams to Mr. and Mrs. William H. Lane, July 15, 1983 (Lane Collection).

ANSEL ADAMS

THE EARLY YEARS

In 1916 two landmark events occurred in the life of Ansel Adams (1902-1984): he traveled with his family to Yosemite National Park for the first time, and his parents gave him a Kodak Box Brownie camera.[1] This summer vacation at once initiated Adams's yearly visits to Yosemite and awakened his interest in photography. His earliest pictures were, in his his own words, simply snapshots taken as "a visual diary of my mountain trips."[2] Adams's immediate enthusiasm for his new hobby led him barely a year later to take a job with local San Francisco photo-finisher Frank Dittman, who taught him the rudiments of film development.

In these initial years of picture making Adams began to show an awareness of expressive and formal qualities beyond the concept of the snapshot. In June 1920 he wrote to his father from Yosemite, analyzing a print he had enclosed in the letter, *Diamond Cascade*: "I want you to see what I am trying to do in pictorial photography — suggestive and impressionistic you may call it — either — it is the representation of material things in the abstract or purely imaginative way."[3] *"Wind,"* of 1919, (pl. 1), is an example of Adams's experimentation, of his first work as an artist rather than a souvenir photographer. Done in the Pictorialist style, the image has an overall soft focus that is enhanced by the warm tones of the richly textured paper on which it is printed.[4] Even the title is romantic and evocative. The accidental quality of snapshot composition is now absent; the curving juniper tree on the far left frames the view to the distant mountain.

The twenties was a period of personal as well as artistic development. Beginning in 1920, Adams spent four summers as caretaker of LaConte Lodge, the Sierra Club's outpost at Yosemite. While scouting around the Yosemite area for a practice piano in 1921, he met Virginia Best, whom he would marry seven years later. Her father, an artist, owned Best's Studio, the park concession where Adams found his piano.

In April 1927 Adams reported having experienced in Yosemite "a personally historic moment in my photographic career," one that reaffirmed his commitment to creative photography. He had made the difficult climb to the Diving Board, a rocky outcropping opposite the cliff face of Half Dome, with Virginia Best and three friends, stopping to make photographs at several points along the way. He described the intellectual processes of photographing the last subject of the trip, Half Dome itself:

> "I began to think about how the print was to appear, and if it would transmit any of the feeling of the monumental shape before me in terms of its expressive-emotional quality. I began to see in my mind's eye the finished print I desired: the brooding cliff with a dark sky and the sharp rendition of distant, snowy Tenaya Peak."[5]

When he developed the plate that evening, he knew he had succeeded: "I had been able to realize a desired image: not the way the subject appeared in reality but how it felt to me and how it must appear in the finished print."

The image which resulted from Adams's "first true visualization" was *Monolith–The Face of Half Dome* (pl. 6). Half Dome is an impressive subject even when taken by an amateur photographer, but Adams carefully manipulated formal elements to create a sublime image in the tradition of the nineteenth-century Romantic landscape photographers and painters. His point of view forces a close confrontation with the monumental, shadowy cliff on the right, producing visual density that is relieved by the snowy and distant view to Tenaya Peak on the left. Adams emphasizes Half Dome's sheer face with the vertical orientation of his composition and by filling up the right half of the picture, leaving just a wedge of sky visible at the top. In *Monolith*, Adams rejected the earlier Pictorialist style for a sharp-focus approach that reveals the specific textures of his subject. Finally, he had learned how to work with light. He patiently waited for the afternoon sun to strike the face of Half Dome, and once it did, he photographed the view through a red filter, which "dramatically darkened the sky and the shadows on the great cliff." The blacks of both sky and upper cliff are virtually the same in value, separated only by the thin line of white snow on the summit of the monolith. This sets up a wholly modern spatial struggle between the flatness of the resulting pattern and the three-dimensionality of the subject. Adams achieved his desired Romantic effect — the hulking monolith of the title — but he did so using a twentieth-century approach like that of the photographs of his contemporaries Charles Sheeler or Edward Weston, or in the paintings of John Marin or Arthur Dove.

Throughout his career Adams continued to print from favorite early negatives. He constantly refined his own technical craft and investigated new advances in the field. Each reprint he made, therefore, varies from the previous ones. In the 1950s Adams experimented with enlarging negatives, and *Monolith–The Face of Half Dome* (pl. 7) was one of the images he redeveloped on this monumental scale. The scope of the Lane Collection allows the rare opportunity to compare examples of each version. More than three times the size of the 1927 print, the later *Monolith* emphasizes very different aspects of the composition. The lack of foreground, for example, with no standing room, now emphasizes the precarious position of the viewer. Half Dome seems even more massive since each tiny tree has become distinct. Adams modified the way he cropped the composition at the upper right, closing out more of the sky, and thus the viewer is presented squarely with the face of the cliff, forced to look up. Finally, by printing the later version on glossy paper, Adams has intensified the contrasts between the lights and darks.

Adams had included *Monolith–The Face of Half Dome* in his first portfolio, "Parmelian Prints of the High Sierras." Published in August 1927, the portfolio was the brainchild of Albert Bender. After viewing Adams's prints one evening at a party, Bender, a San Francisco businessman and art patron, invited the photographer to his office where they planned the project. It was the first interest anyone outside had shown in Adams's work. The term "Parmelian Print," apparently derived from parmelia, a genus of mountain lichen, was invented by the publisher, Jean Chambers Moore, and Adams himself, believing it would be more marketable than simply "photograph," since the medium was not generally considered a fine art. Adams always regretted this breach of faith in photography as an artistic medium.[6]

"Parmelian Prints of the High Sierras" provides a summary of Adams's first decade of photography. In it Adams reprinted on textured paper his earlier negatives, from 1919 right up to the year of the publication, including some Pictorialist work, but emphasizing sharp-focus images. As the title indicates, the eighteen prints are all landscapes, which had been Adams's primary subject up to this time, with the exception of occasional shots of family and friends. Taken as a whole, the photographs underscore one theme that Adams would pursue throughout his career: the quiet grandeur of nature untouched by man. Both *Monolith–The Face of Half Dome* and *Glacier Point* (pls. 6, 7 and 2), for example, present Adams's view of a pristine wilderness. At the same time, his photographs continue a nineteenth-century tradition of showing the American West as the Garden of Eden. In Yosemite, this theme goes back to the paintings of Albert Bierstadt and the photographs of Carleton Watkins and Eadweard Muybridge.

Adams married Virginia Best on January 2, 1928. The following spring he was asked to join the annual summer Sierra

Club outing in the Canadian Rockies, for the first time as official photographer. A number of prints resulted from the trip, including the shadowy, yet angled peaks of *From Moose Pass* (pl. 4). That same year the Sierra Club held Adams's first one-man exhibition in San Francisco. Also in 1928, Albert Bender introduced Adams to Edward Weston. Adams's initial response to Weston's prints was mixed: "They were the first work of such serious quality I had ever seen, but surprisingly I did not immediately understand or even like them; I thought them hard and mannered."[7]

By 1931, however, Adams wrote a positive review of Weston's one-man show at the M.H. DeYoung Memorial Museum in San Francisco for *The Fortnightly*.[8] In the intervening years Adams's photography had begun to show some of Weston's influence, but it always retained a quality peculiarly Adams's own: he walked a tightrope between his modernist approach and his often romantic subjects. In *Rocks, Baker's Beach*, (pl. 9), for example, Adams has chosen a "Weston" subject, but rather than entirely closing in on the object as a natural abstraction, Adams kept the rocks identifiable and focused instead on the subtle differences of sunlight dancing over the wet and dry surfaces. Or, in *Snow on Trees, Yosemite Valley* (pl. 8), a subject more characteristically his own, Adams manipulated the range of the whites of the light on the snow against the crisscrossing branches of pine.

Throughout the 1920s Adams had struggled with the question of whether to pursue photography as a profession or to continue studying piano, which he had taken up seriously in 1914. Albert Bender's critical encouragement in the late twenties had helped direct Adams back to photography, but he continued to waver between the two careers. His internal battle came to an end in 1930, when he met Paul Strand on a trip to Taos, New Mexico. After viewing Strand's "glorious negatives"[9] Adams made his decision: from now on he would devote himself to creative photography.

To earn a living, Adams started accepting commercial assignments, ranging from department store catalogues and advertisements to portraiture. Like Weston and Strand, he began to print exclusively on glossy papers at about this time, and in 1932, he joined with Weston, Imogen Cunningham, Willard Van Dyke, Sonya Noskowiak and others to form Group f/64. Named for the small lens aperture used for sharpness and depth, Group f/64 advocated straight photography — as Adams described, "photographs that looked like photographs, not imitations of other art forms."[10]

The philosophy of Group f/64 endured far longer than the formal association itself. Only two exhibitions were ever organized, the initial one at the DeYoung Museum in 1932 and the other in 1933 at the newly-opened Ansel Adams Gallery in San Francisco.[11] Adams included *"Minerva" from Sutro Gardens* (pl. 13) in the last Group f/64 exhibition in 1933. Printed on glossy paper and shot in sharp focus, *"Minerva"* exemplifies the visual ideals of Group f/64. The handling of bright sunlight and deep shadow across the statue's body, and the choice of a romantic subject, however, are Adams hallmarks. The highlights on the sculpture are picked up again in the bright whites in the distant surf. Adams almost fills the vertical composition with the gentle backwards s-curve of Minerva's form, placing her slightly to the right of center to open a vista to the ocean. Her shape is balanced by the sloping diagonal of the road below and by the misty horizon line. In the hands of a Pictorialist, the subject would have become sentimental, but Adams clearly shows his concerns with modern formal issues while still allowing Minerva to be appealing in her romantic decay.

Adams achieves a similarly delicate balance of subject and style in his Shipwreck Series (pls. 11 and 12), made in the early thirties. He photographed the deteriorating remains of sunken vessels that had washed up on the coast near Land's End at the mouth of San Francisco Bay.[12] While the idea of a series, and even the close-up views, may have been suggested by the work of Edward Weston, Adams once again takes his own route. The shipwreck theme has a long history of representation by Romantic artists. Here, without the titles, the subjects would be largely unrecognizable. Some, such as *Shipwreck Series #1, Steel and Stone* (pl. 11), are still difficult to see even once the subject is known. A mysterious object in the shape of a bicycle seat seems to be suspended without support, centered in the composition. Adams, through light and focus, has matched the texture of the corroded steel to that of the surrounding rocks. Light hits the right side of the curved wedge shape, and illuminates a triangular patch of rock immediately behind, mimicking the shape, texture and value of the corroded steel. The objects are distinguished only by the sharper edge of the shipwreck, as defined by light. Similarly, the highlight of the upper edge of the steel separates it from the wall of rock in the background. Another highlight, visible through the round hole in the center of the piece from the shipwreck, further complicates the spatial relationships — is this the curved interior of the steel or a continuation of the rock to the right?

Shipwreck Series #1, Steel and Stone may be the only vintage print from the series in existence. When reassembling Adams's 1936 An American Place exhibition in 1982, Andrea Gray, even with the artist's help, could not locate a single vintage photograph from the series.[13] William H. Lane had purchased *Shipwreck Series #1, Steel and Stone* from Adams in 1968 at the same time he ordered from Adams new prints of the whole series (see pl. 12). Adams apparently had difficulty in printing the negatives up to his personal standards, for on July 5, 1972 he wrote Lane, "I made a Surf Sequence and a Shipwreck Sequence for you and they STANK! Everything went dead!! I would like to accuse the paper, but I guess it was just ME!"[14] The new prints were finally delivered in May 1973, accompanied by a letter dated the 17th: "Here are the SURF SEQUENCE and the SHIPWRECK SERIES PRINTS...The Shipwreck Sequence is really a SERIES — it never had any sequence."[15]

In March 1933 Ansel and Virginia Adams traveled cross country to New York City for the first time. Adams's destination was An American Place, the gallery owned by Alfred Stieglitz, champion of modern art and, especially, photography. Adams felt he was ready to consult Stieglitz for a critique of his photographs. After a characteristically brusque initial encounter, Stieglitz responded positively to Adams's work at their second meeting, telling Adams that his photographs ranked with "the finest prints I have ever seen,"[16] and complimented them as "straight."[17] Stieglitz also, according to Virginia Adams, appreciated Adams's technical skill.[18] As a result, Adams and Stieglitz began a serious written exchange of ideas that ended only with Stieglitz's death in 1946. Adams would visit New York and Stieglitz almost annually, bringing his current prints for Stieglitz to study. "Rather than say Stieglitz influenced me in my work," Adams summed up in his autobiography, "I would say that he revealed me to myself. Paul Strand's work showed me the potential of photography as an art form; Stieglitz gave me the confidence that I could express myself through that art form."[19]

The East Coast trip produced two other important results that year: the September opening of the Ansel Adams Gallery in San Francisco as a forum for Group f/64, and in November, his first New York exhibition at Delphic Studios, an important venue for contemporary photography. Three years later in 1936, after several other one-man shows across the country and the publication of his first technical book, *Making a Photograph*, Adams's photographs were finally exhibited by Stieglitz at An American Place.[20]

As the "Parmelian Prints of the High Sierras" had surveyed Adams's work of the 1920s, the exhibition at An American Place reviewed Adams's career as a photographer since his 1930 decision to turn professional. It is surprising to note that of the forty-five photographs in the show, only four were landscapes. Most of the subjects were details and close-up views of natural and manmade objects — pine cones, tree trunks, picket fences and gravestones. One of the prints in the Shipwreck Series was shown.[21] These subjects certainly reflected Adams's involvement with Group f/64, but by including examples of commercial and creative portraiture, as well as architecture and hybrid landscapes like *Cross, San Rafael, California* (pl. 10) he clearly demonstrated his desire not to be categorized. In a brief essay printed with the checklist for the exhibition, he wrote:

> "Photography is a way of telling what you feel about what you see . . . Perception, visualization, and execution are rigorously interrelated; each in itself has little meaning. A competent technique is quite essential in photography, and an adequate and precise apparatus also, but without the elements of imaginative vision and taste the most perfect technical photograph is a vacuous shell."[22]

Throughout the 1930s Adams continued to experiment with a range of subjects. His sense of humor is demonstrated in *Discussion in Art* (pl. 15). In the foreground, two men in business suits are engaged in earnest conversation. In a painting behind them, the figure of the Virgin Mary seems to be participating in the discussion. The Virgin Mary and the men are each represented roughly half length and are the same height and scale. The hand of the man on the left grabs the lapel of the man on the right and his gesture is echoed by the placement of the Virgin's hand over her heart. Finally, since Adams executed the image in black and white, there is a similarity in tone that further blurs the distinction between the painting and the real.

Adams's creative portraiture of the 1930s is exemplified by *Charis Weston* (pl. 19), taken on a trip to the Yosemite high country that Adams took with Edward Weston and Charis Wilson Weston. The portrait's casual snapshot-like effect belies Adams's modernist interest in formal concerns. He filled the vertical composition with Charis's form and shot the image from below, emphasizing the shadows in the neutral light. He repeats shapes such as the curve of the turban (worn as protection against mosquitoes) and the folds of the sweater at the abdomen. These shadows and lines vie with the sitter for visual dominance.

Ansel Adams is not generally associated with cityscapes, especially those of New York. But *R.C.A. Building, New York* (pl. 23) demonstrates that Adams could adapt his style to subjects both physically and spiritually removed from Yosemite. The forceful shape of the skyscraper here is flattened both by the point of view and the natural light coming from behind the building. The shorter structures in the foreground are cast into deeper shadows of rich blacks, but a tiny white dot of a street light relieves this darkness in the lower left. Adams once again conducts a constant dialogue between the three-dimensional reality of the represented objects and the two-dimensional pattern of his art.

In 1939 Adams met the photography critics Beaumont and Nancy Newhall in New York. When they visited San Francisco for the first time in 1940, Adams drove them to Carmel to meet Edward Weston. On the drive back to the city the trio stopped to take pictures at several points along the way.

Adams described the evolution of Surf Sequence (cat. nos. 61-65, pl. 21):

> "I photographed from a cliff top, directing my camera almost straight down to the surf patterns washing upon the beach below in a continuing sequence of beautiful images. As I became aware of the relations between the changing light and surf, I began making exposure after exposure."[23]

Although Adams acknowledged that each of the Surf Sequence photographs could stand on its own, he conceded that "a group of five displayed together has the greatest effect."[24] The sequence did not, however, have a prescribed order, as Adams wrote to William H. Lane after he finished printing a set for Lane in 1973, "The Surf Sequence can really be put in any sequence you feel right."[25]

In each of the Surf Sequence images Adams's "straight down" view of the shore flattens the natural depth in the landscape. Here, more than in any other composition, pattern dominates in horizontal bands of varying values. The actual representation remains recognizable, but subordinate. In addition to his ongoing formal experiments, Adams innovatively depicted the concept of change (through movement and the passage of time), by the comparison of one Surf Sequence photograph to any other or to them all.[26]

Adams's most prolific and perhaps best-known decade of photography began in 1940. During the forties Adams began to produce such heroic landscapes as *Moonrise, Hernandez, New Mexico*, 1941, (cat. no. 69), which by their sheer beauty alone would become his signature works. At the same time, in their formalist concern with line and tone and their romantic subject matter, these images show they are clearly based in the early experiments of the 1920s and 1930s.

KAREN E. QUINN

Notes

1. The chronology consulted for this essay was researched by James Alinder and published in Mary Street Alinder and Andrea Gray Stillman, eds., *Ansel Adams Letters and Images 1916-1984*, (Boston, 1988), pp. 391-394, henceforth referred to as *Letters*. According to Virginia Adams (interview with Theodore E. Stebbins, Jr., and Karen E. Quinn, May 18, 1991) this is the most accurate chronology of Ansel Adams's life and career.
2. Ansel Adams with Mary Street Alinder, *Ansel Adams An Autobiography*, (Boston, 1985), p. 69, henceforth referred to as *Autobiography*.
3. *Letters*, p. 7.
4. The photograph is printed on Dassonville Paper.
5. *Autobiography*, pp. 75-76.
6. Ibid., p. 82.
7. Ibid., p. 237.
8. Ibid., p. 238.
9. Ibid., p. 109.
10. Ibid., p. 110. Adams did, however, manipulate his prints.
11. Ibid., p. 115. Adams' association with the gallery was brief — under a year. He founded the gallery after his 1933 trip to New York to "reflect the aesthetic stance of An American Place (Alfred Stieglitz's gallery) and Group f/64 as well."
12. Andrea Gray, *Ansel Adams An American Place*, 1936, (Tucson, 1982), plate 44, henceforth referred to as *An American Place*.
13. Ibid., plate 44.
14. Letter from Ansel Adams to William H. Lane, July 5, 1972 (Lane Collection).
15. Unpublished letter from Ansel Adams to William H. Lane, May 17, 1973 (Lane Collection).
16. *An American Place*, p. 13.
17. *Autobiography*, p. 125.
18. Interview with Virginia Adams by Theodore E. Stebbins, Jr., and Karen E. Quinn, May 18, 1991.
19. *Autobiography*, p. 126.
20. *An American Place*, is invaluable in recreating this seminal exhibition, October 27 - November 25, 1936.
21. Which specific image from the Shipwreck Series is undetermined, see *An American Place*, plate 44. Also included in the 1936 exhibition were *Anchors*, cat. no. 22, *Museum Storeroom*, cat. no. 35 and *Grass and Burned Stump*, cat. no. 47.
22. *An American Place*, p. 39. The entire checklist and essay are reproduced in facsimile.
23. *Autobiography*, pp. 199-200.
24. Ibid., p. 200.
25. Letter by Ansel Adams to William H. Lane, May 17, 1973 (Lane Collection).
26. James Alinder, "Ansel Adams, American Artist," in James Alinder and Nicolai Cikovsky, Jr., *Ansel Adams: Classic Images The Museum Set*, (Boston, 1985), p. 16.

PLATES

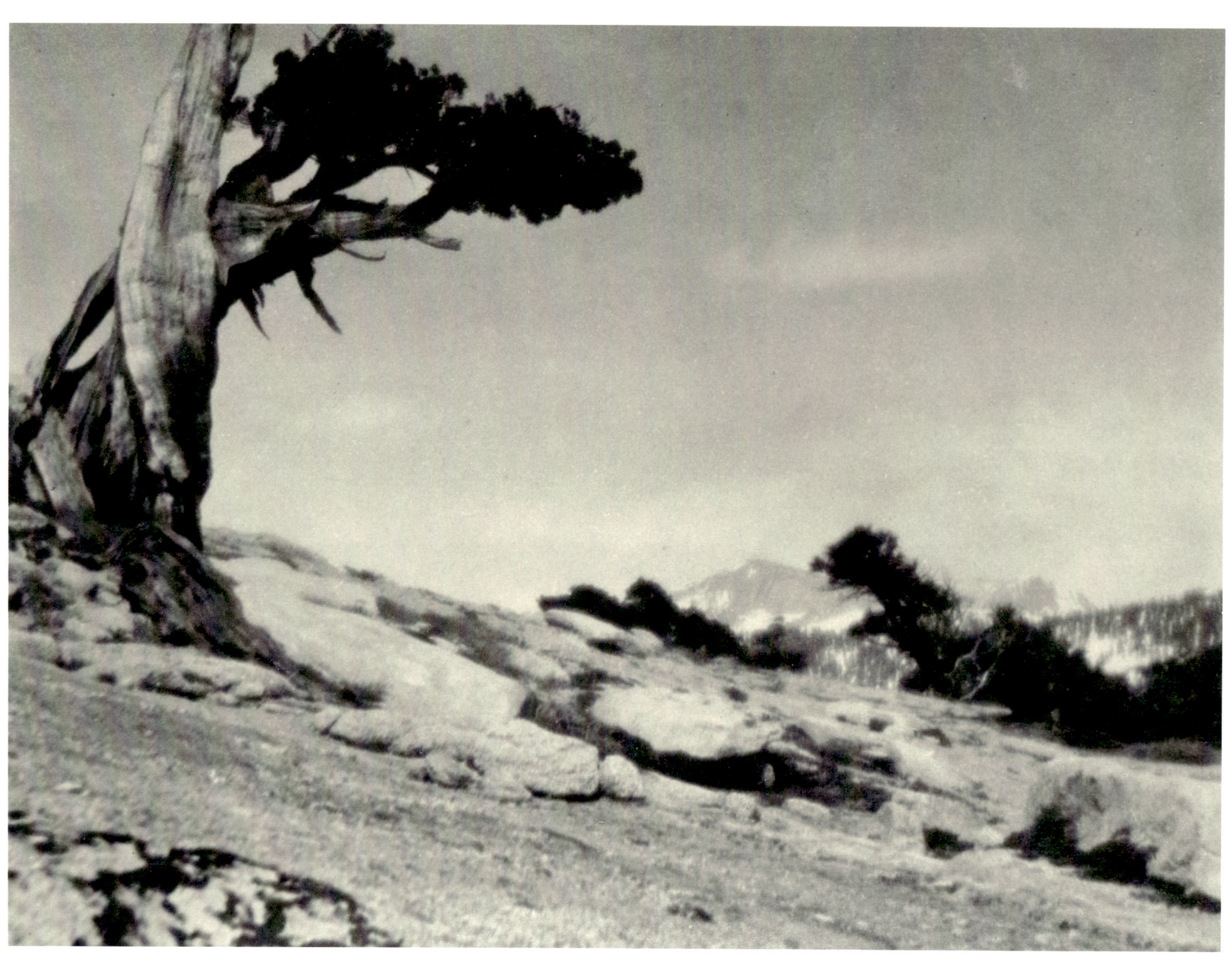

Plate 1 (cat. no. 1). *"Wind,"* about 1919.

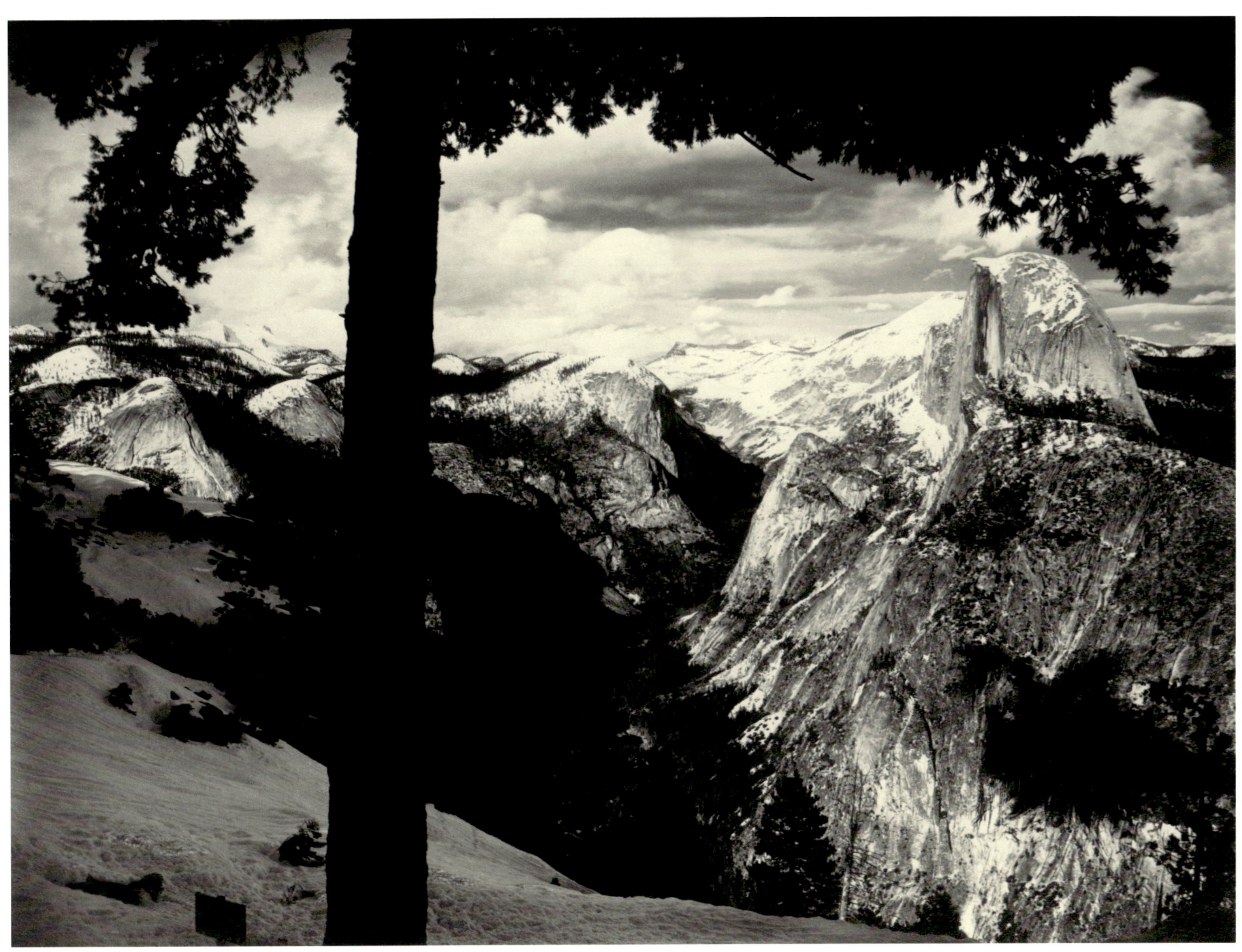

Plate 2 (cat. no. 3). *Glacier Point,* 1927.

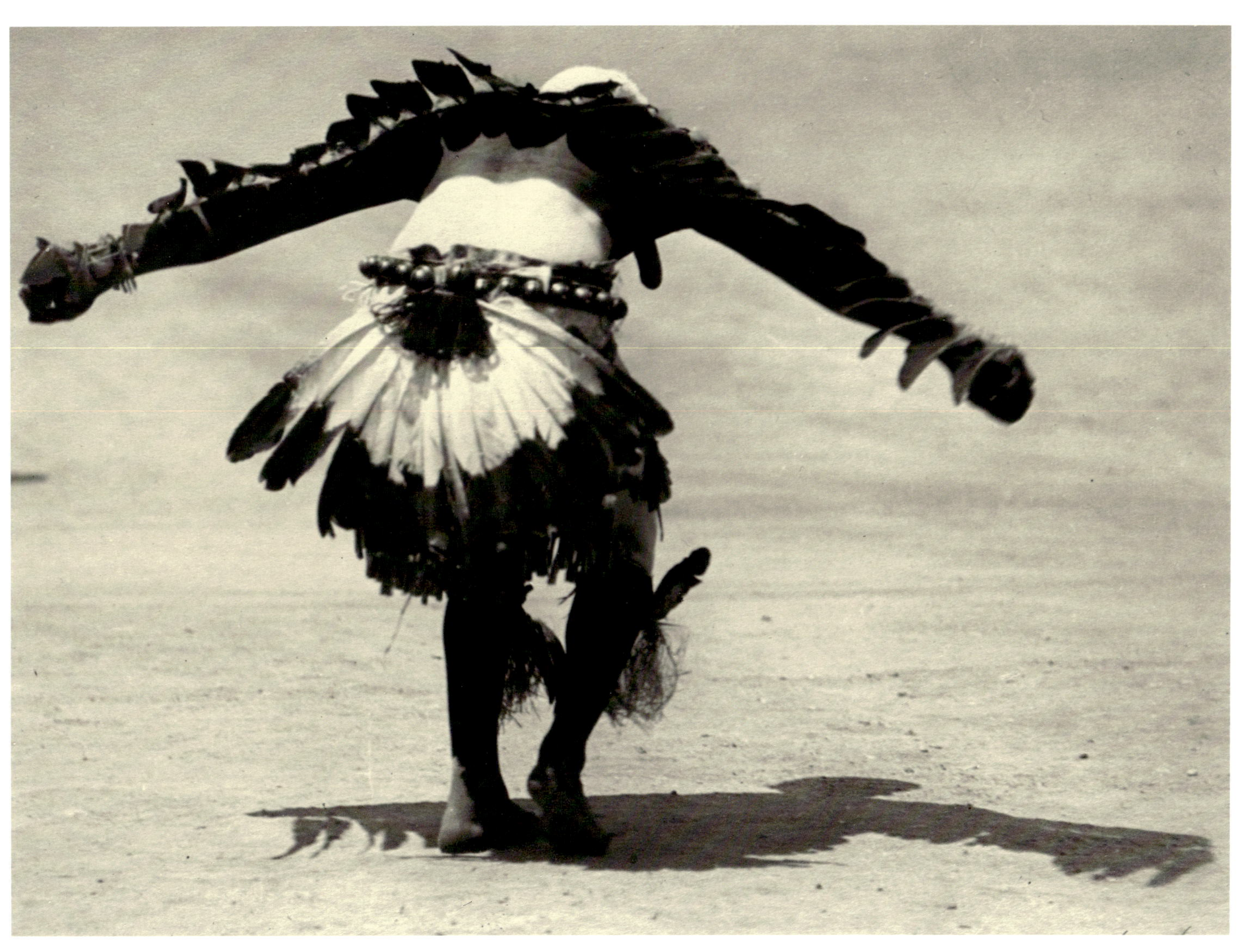

Plate 3 (cat. no. 11). *Eagle Dance*, about 1928-9.

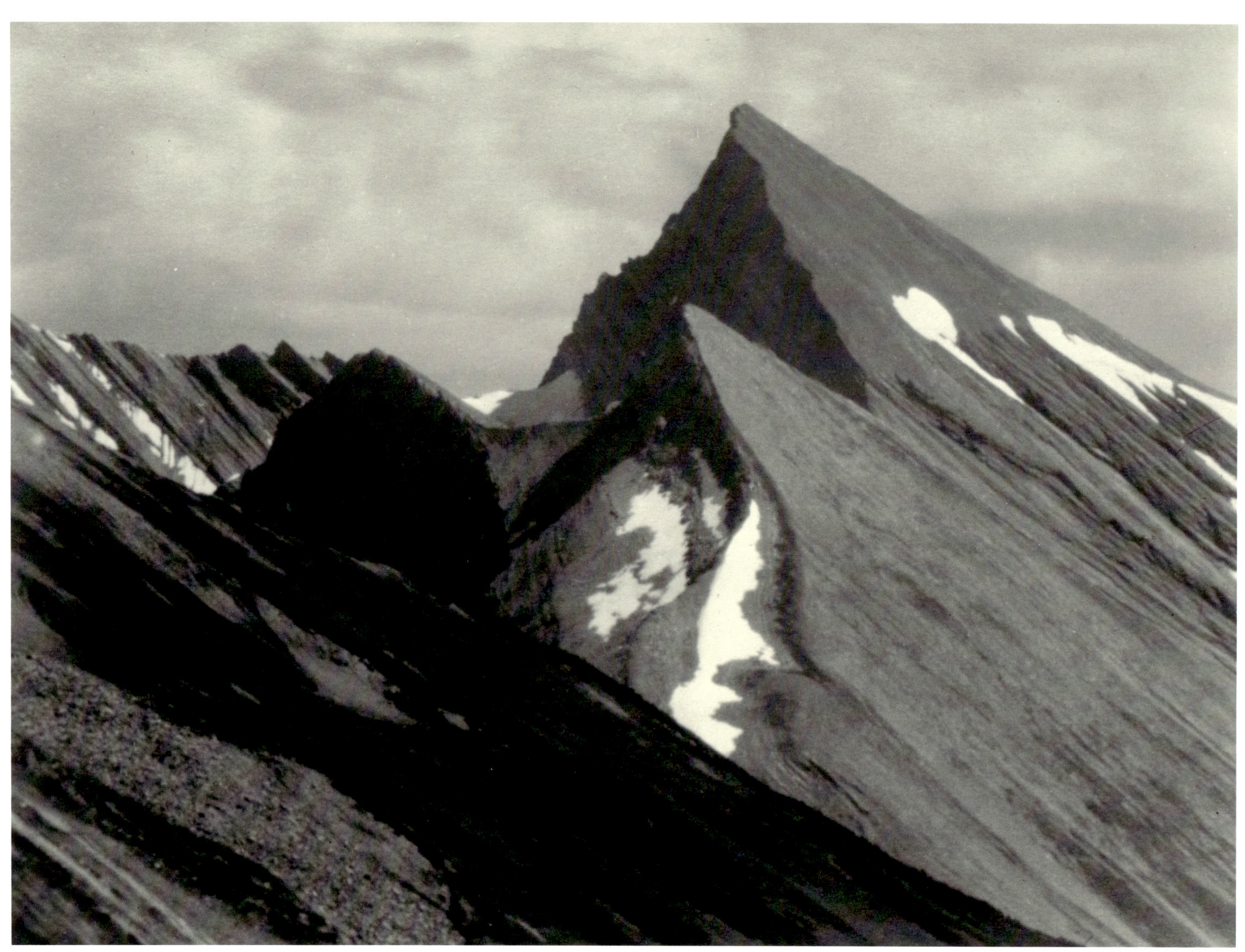

Plate 4 (cat. no. 9). *From Moose Pass*, 1928.

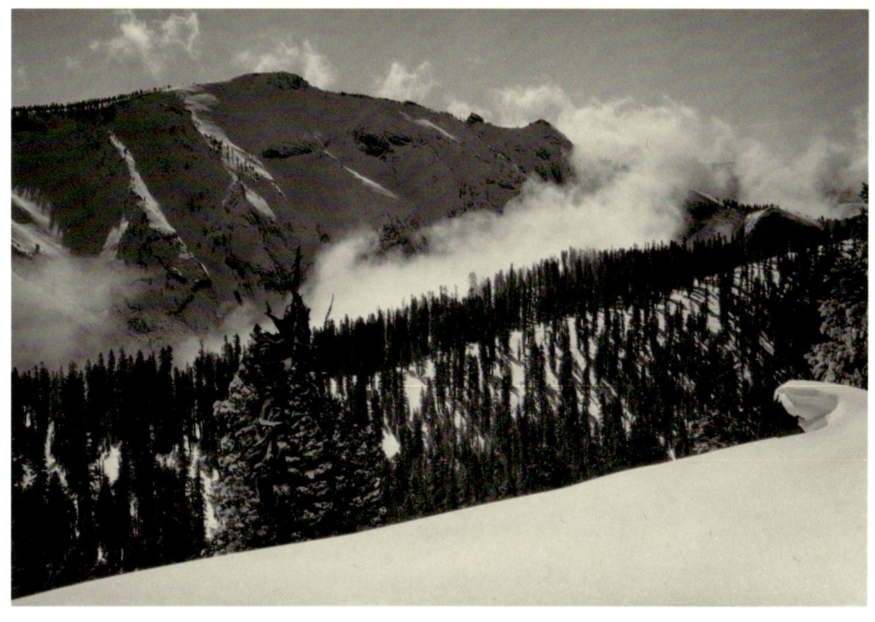

Plate 5 (cat. no. 12). *From near Mt. Watkins, Winter, Yosemite National Park*, negative 1929, print 1930-1932.

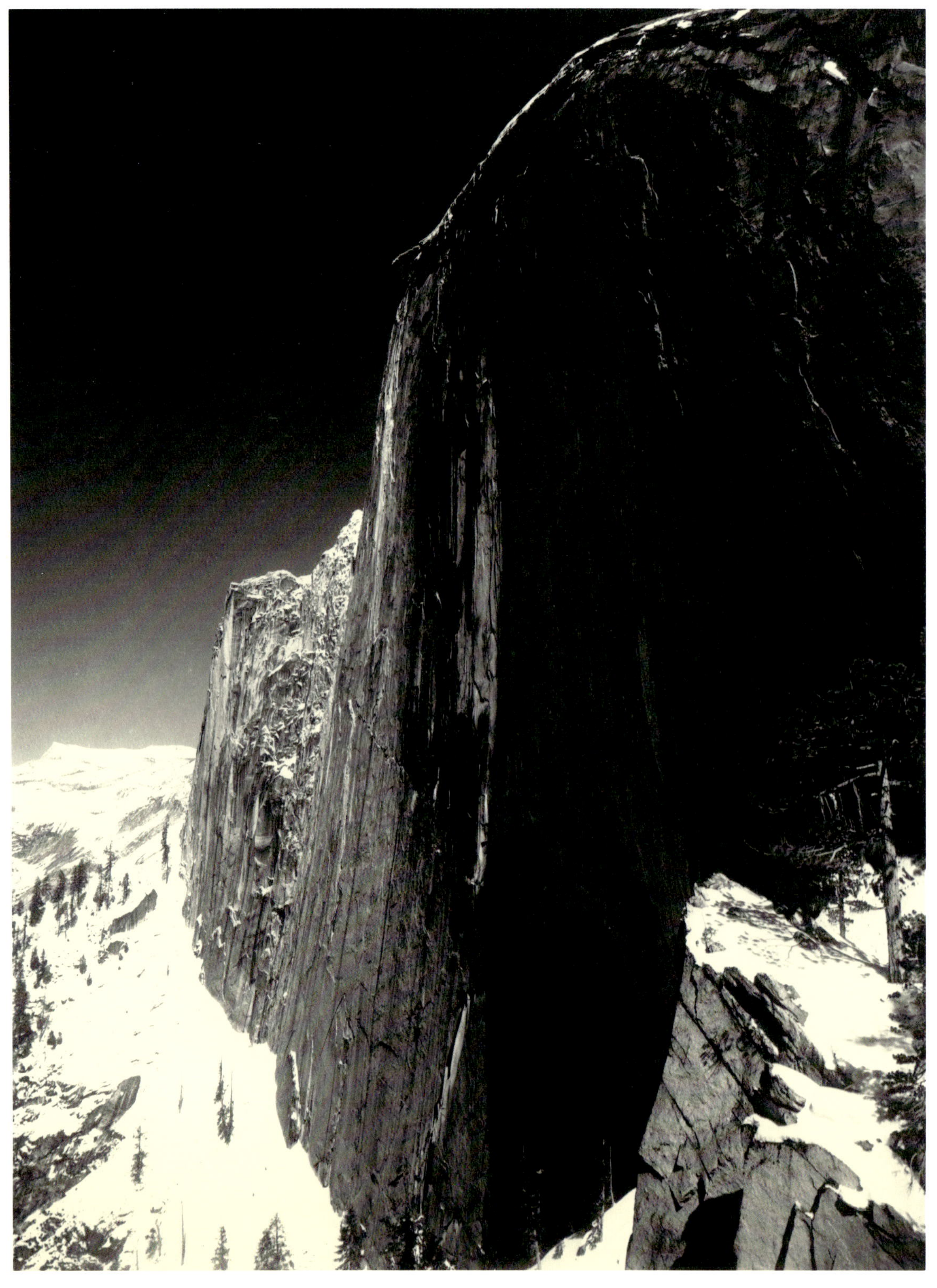

Plate 6 (cat. no. 7). *Monolith—The Face of Half Dome*, 1927.

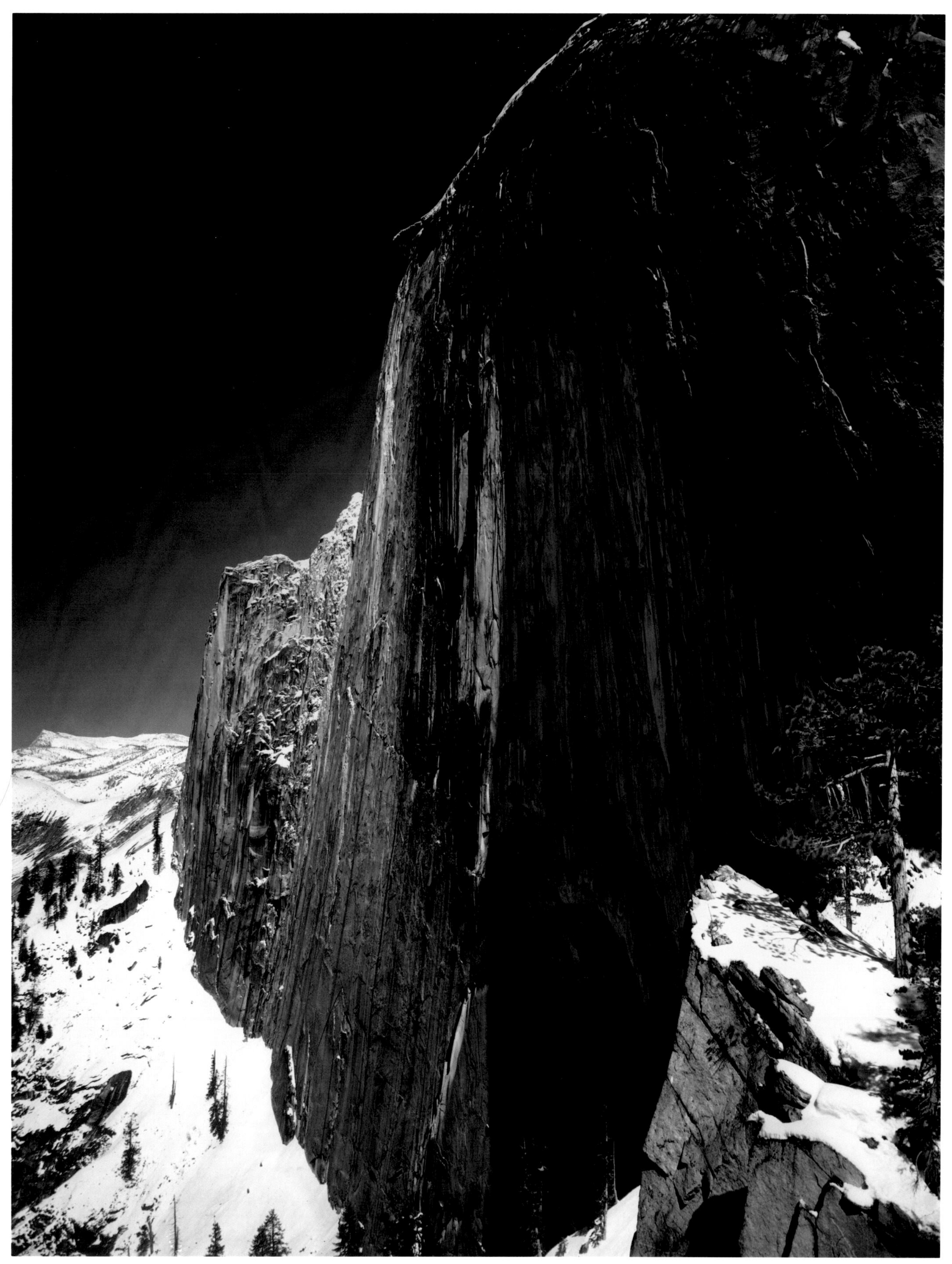

Plate 7 (cat. no. 8). *Monolith — The Face of Half Dome*, negative 1927, print 1950-60.

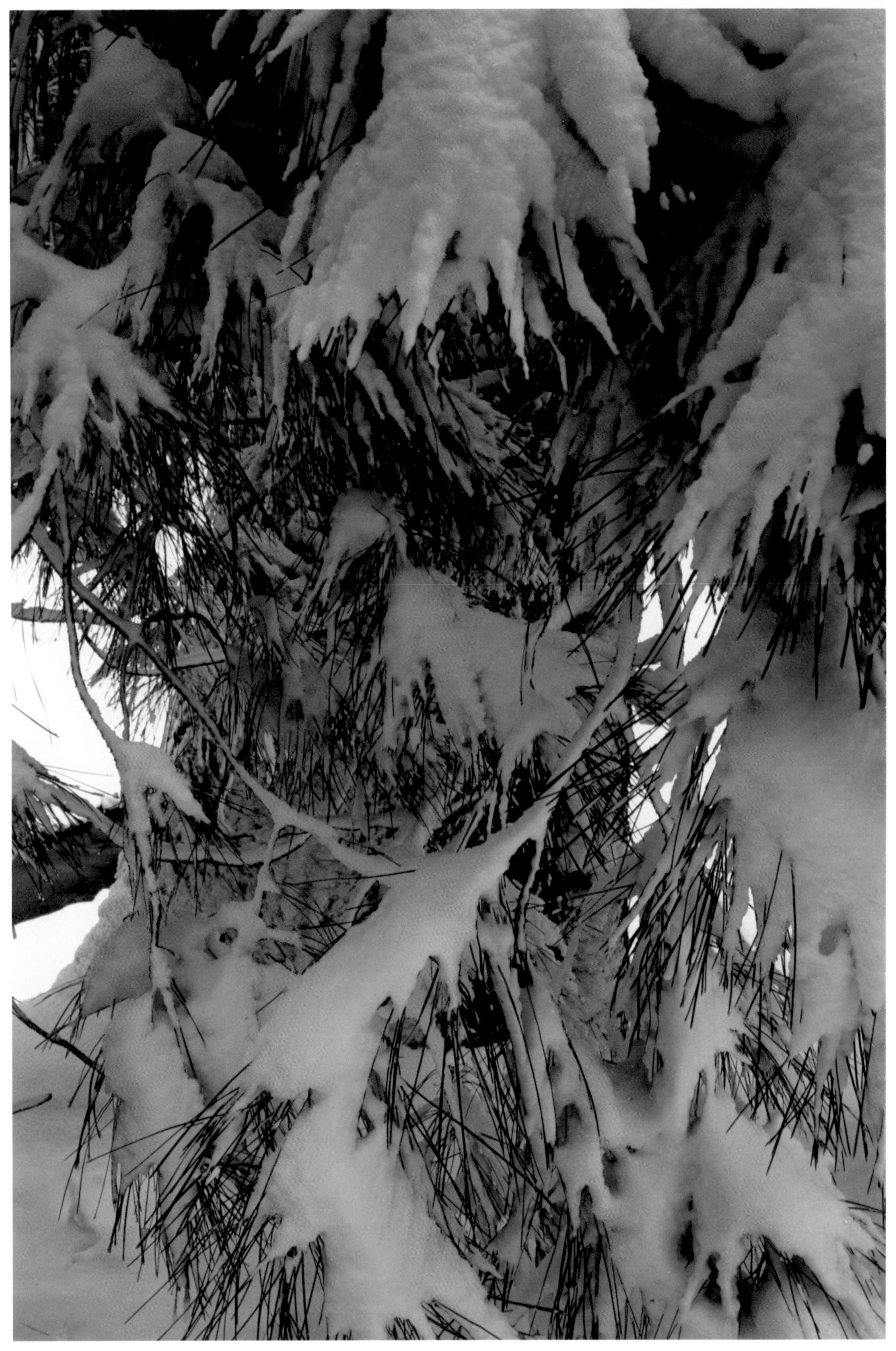

Plate 8 (cat. no. 16). *Snow on Trees, Yosemite Valley,* about 1930.

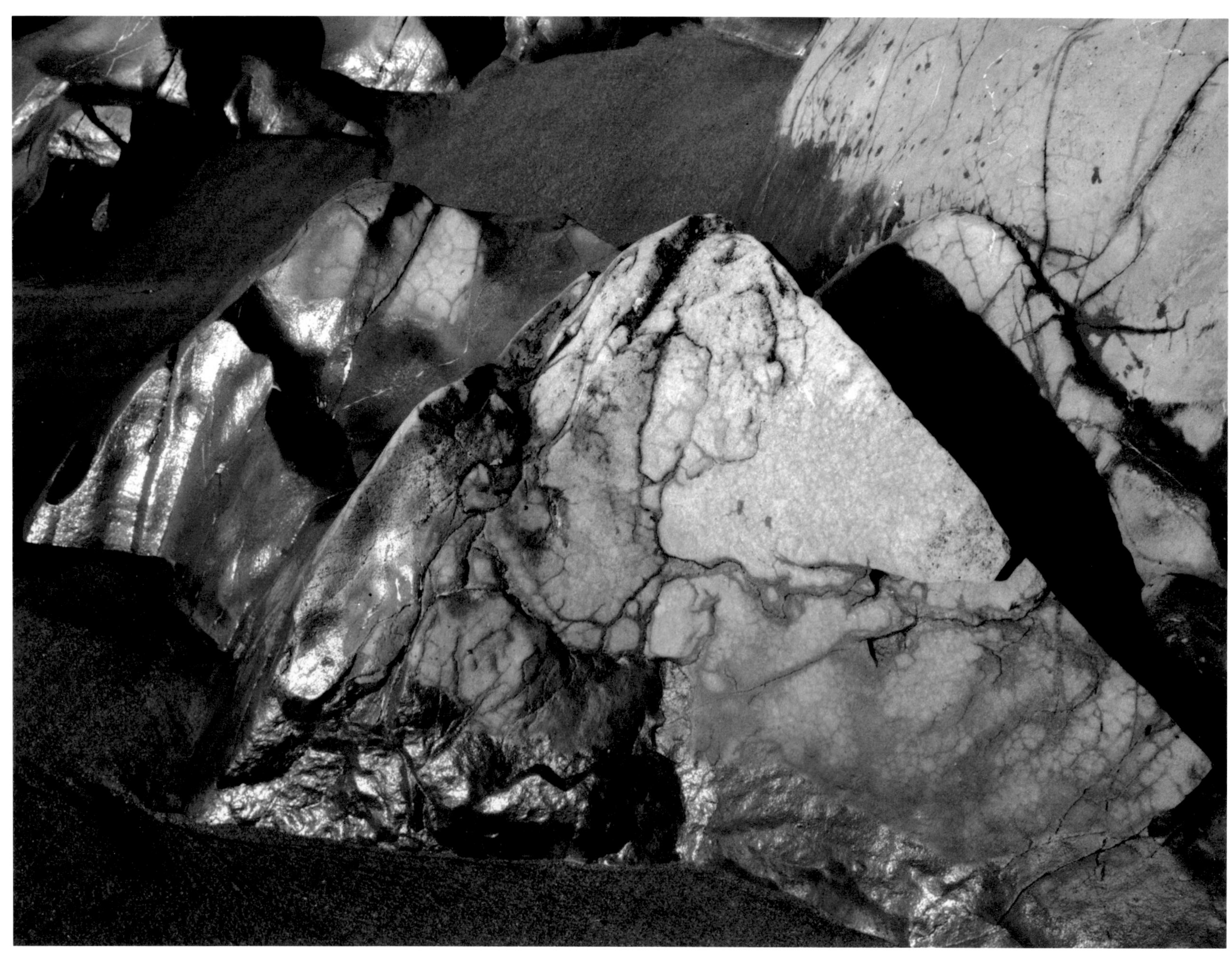

Plate 9 (cat. no. 17). *Rocks, Baker's Beach, San Francisco*, about 1931.

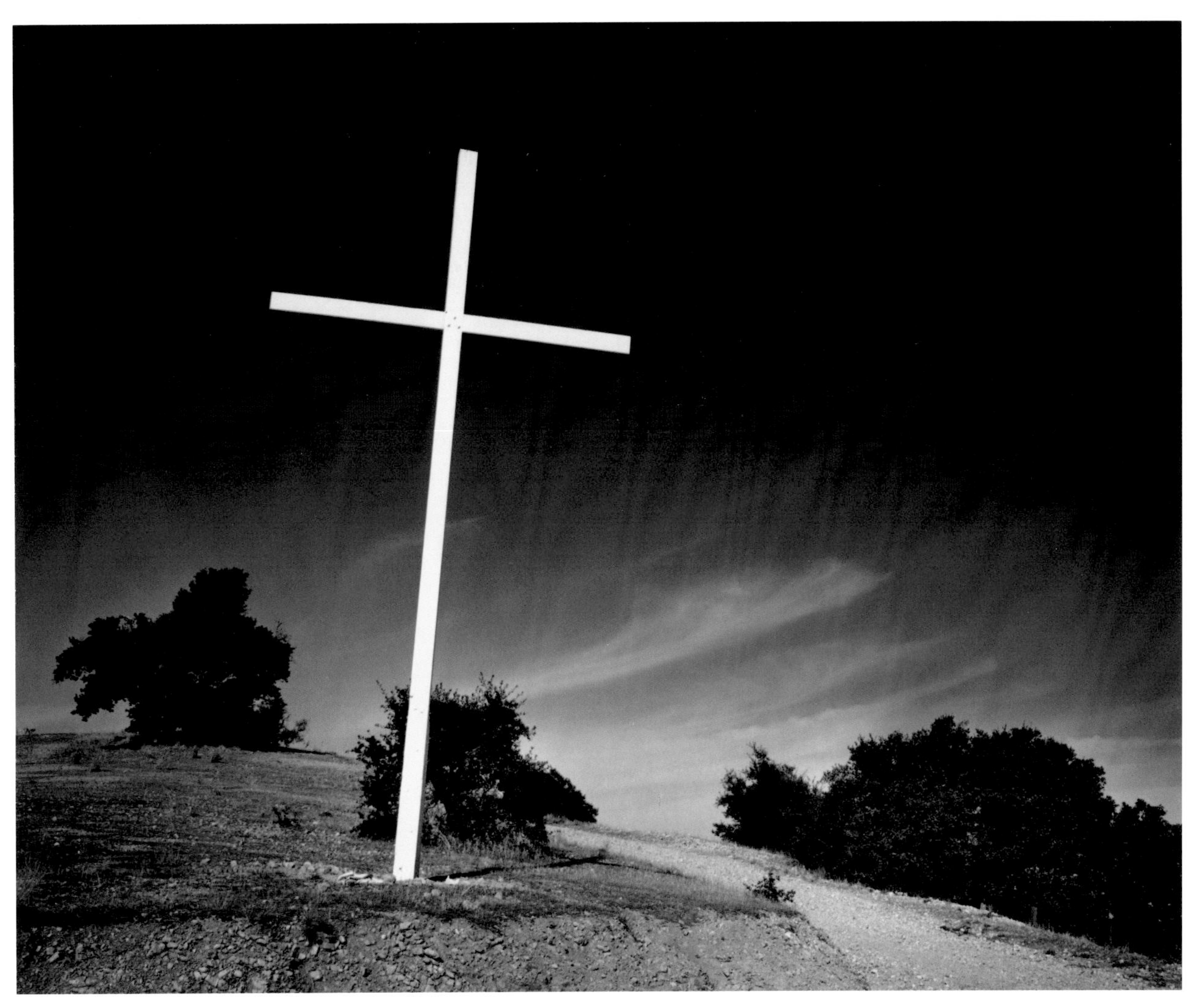

Plate 10 (cat. no. 18). *Cross, San Rafael, California,* 1932.

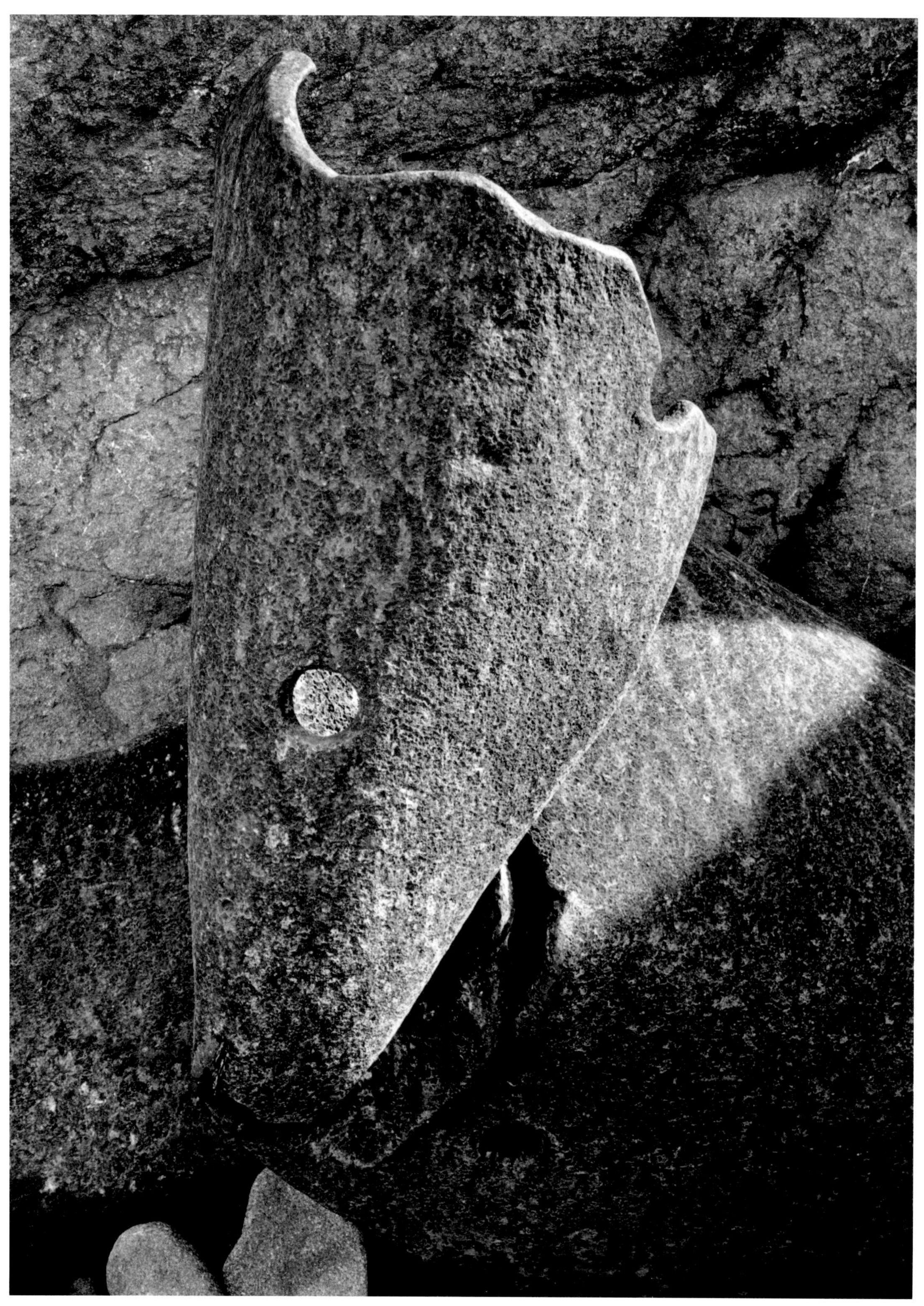

Plate 11 (cat. no. 23). *Shipwreck Series #1, Steel and Stone,* about 1932.

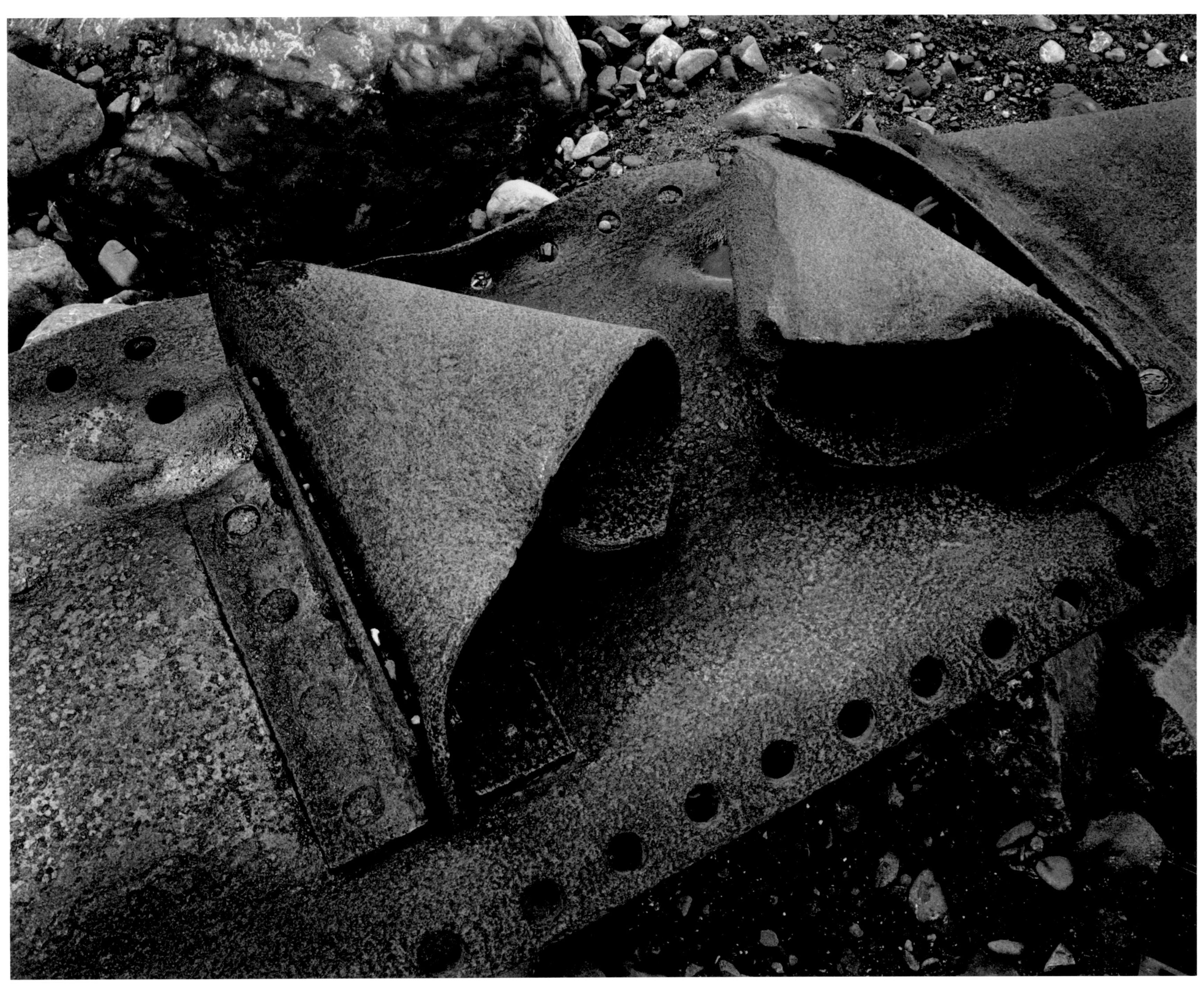

Plate 12 (cat. no. 25). *Shipwreck Series*, negative about 1932, print about 1973.

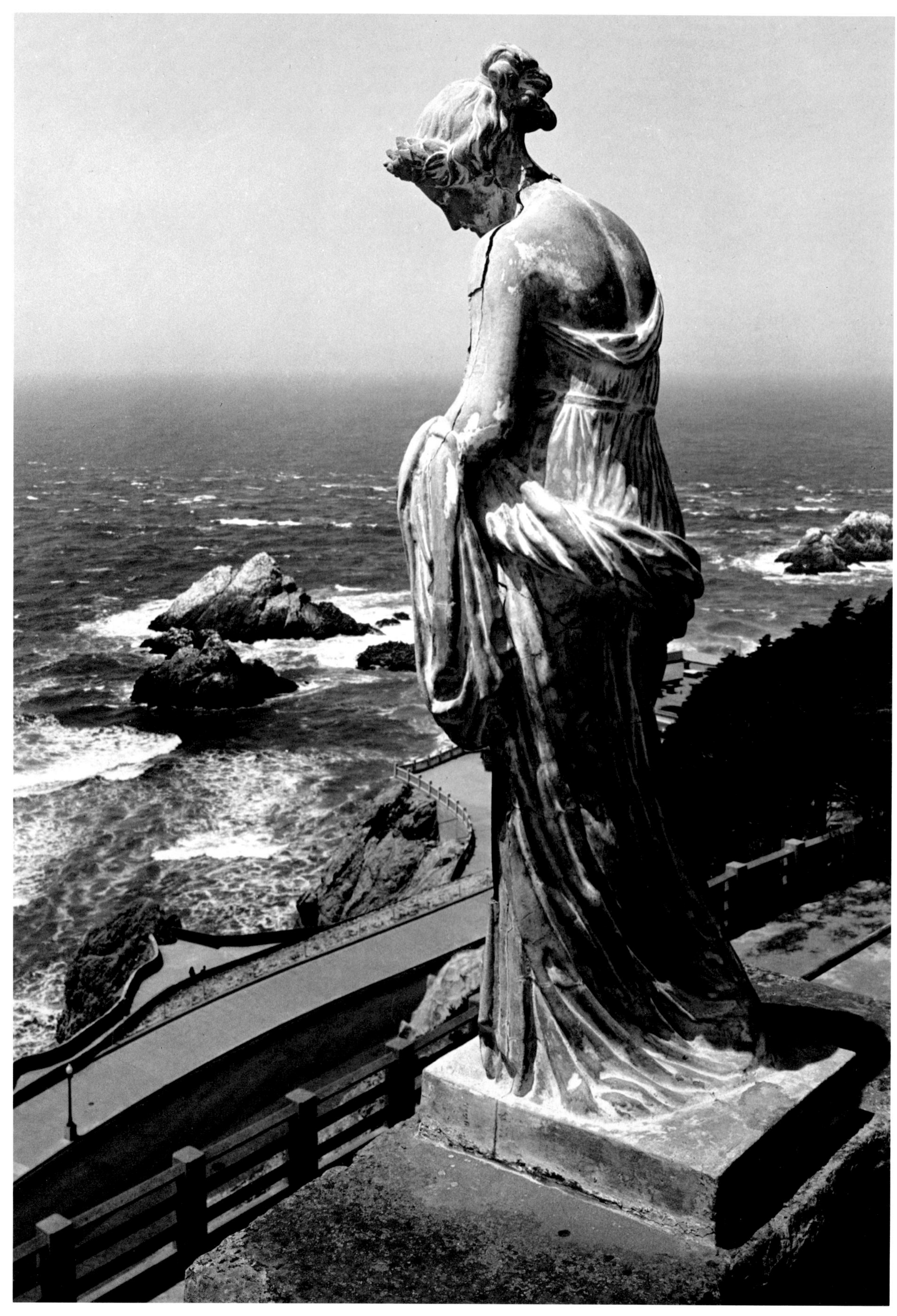

Plate 13 (cat. no. 29). *"Minerva" from Sutro Gardens, San Francisco,* 1933.

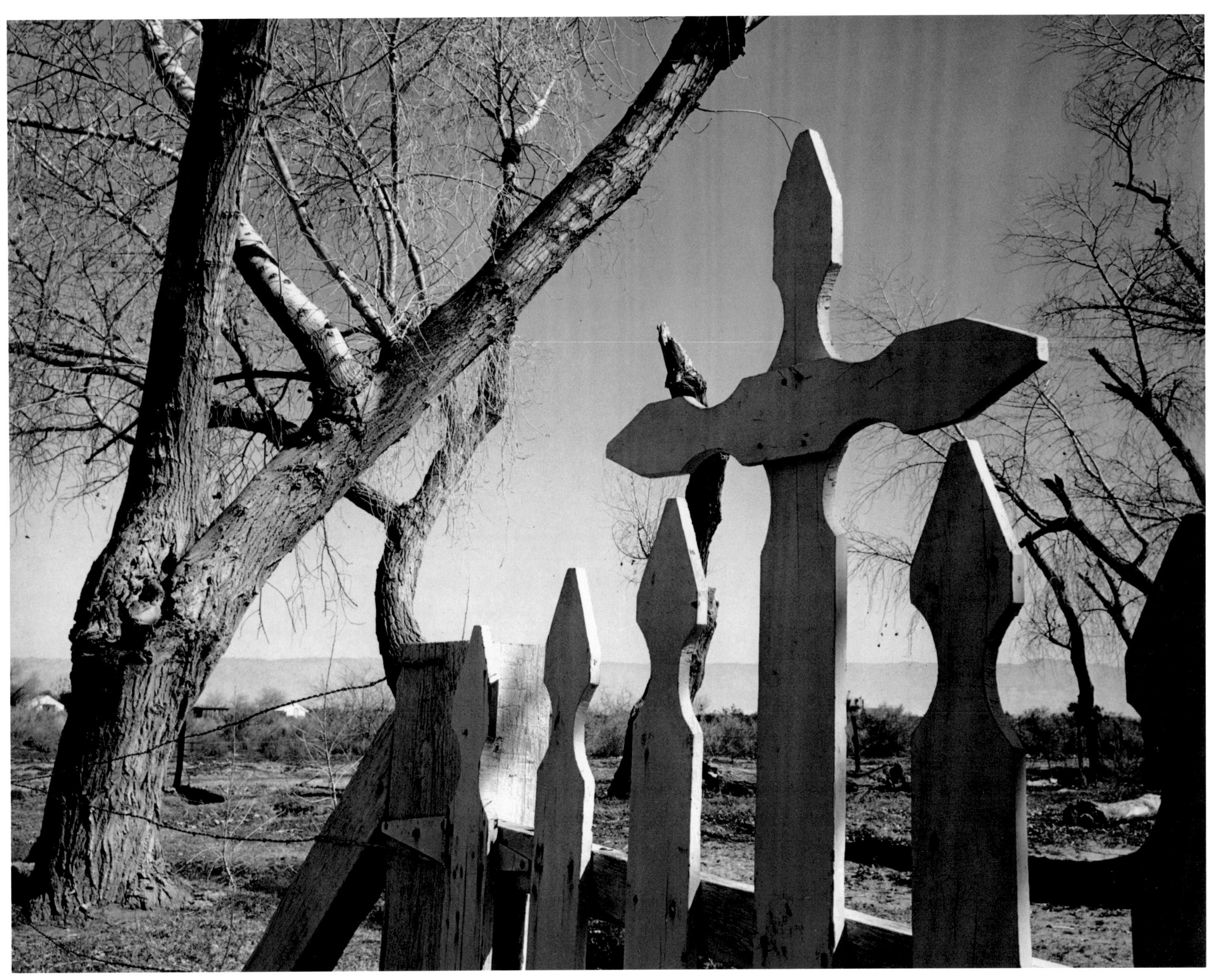

Plate 14 (cat. no. 33). *Mexican Section, Palm Springs, California*, negative about 1934, print about 1935.

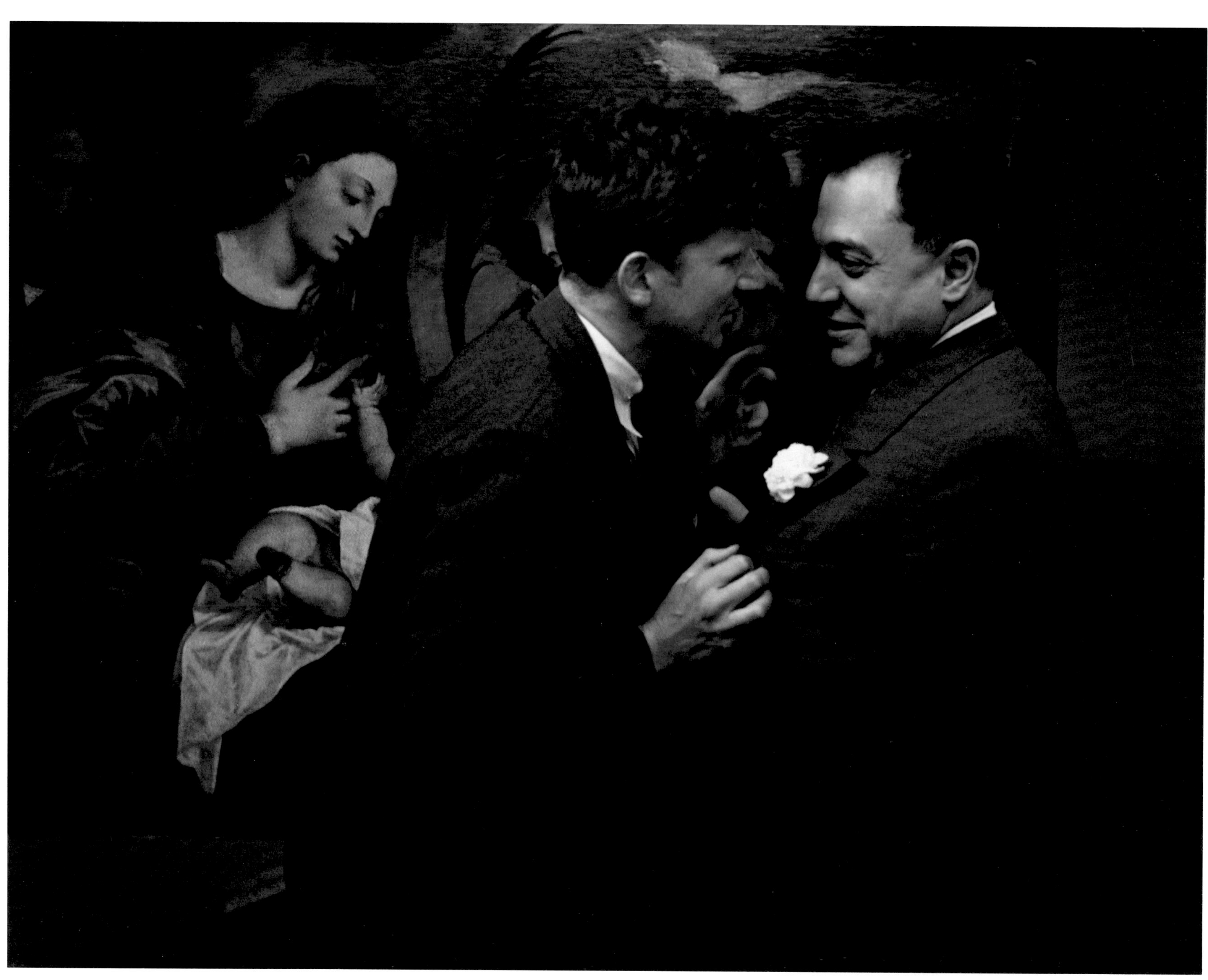

Plate 15 (cat. no. 38). *Discussion in Art*, about 1935.

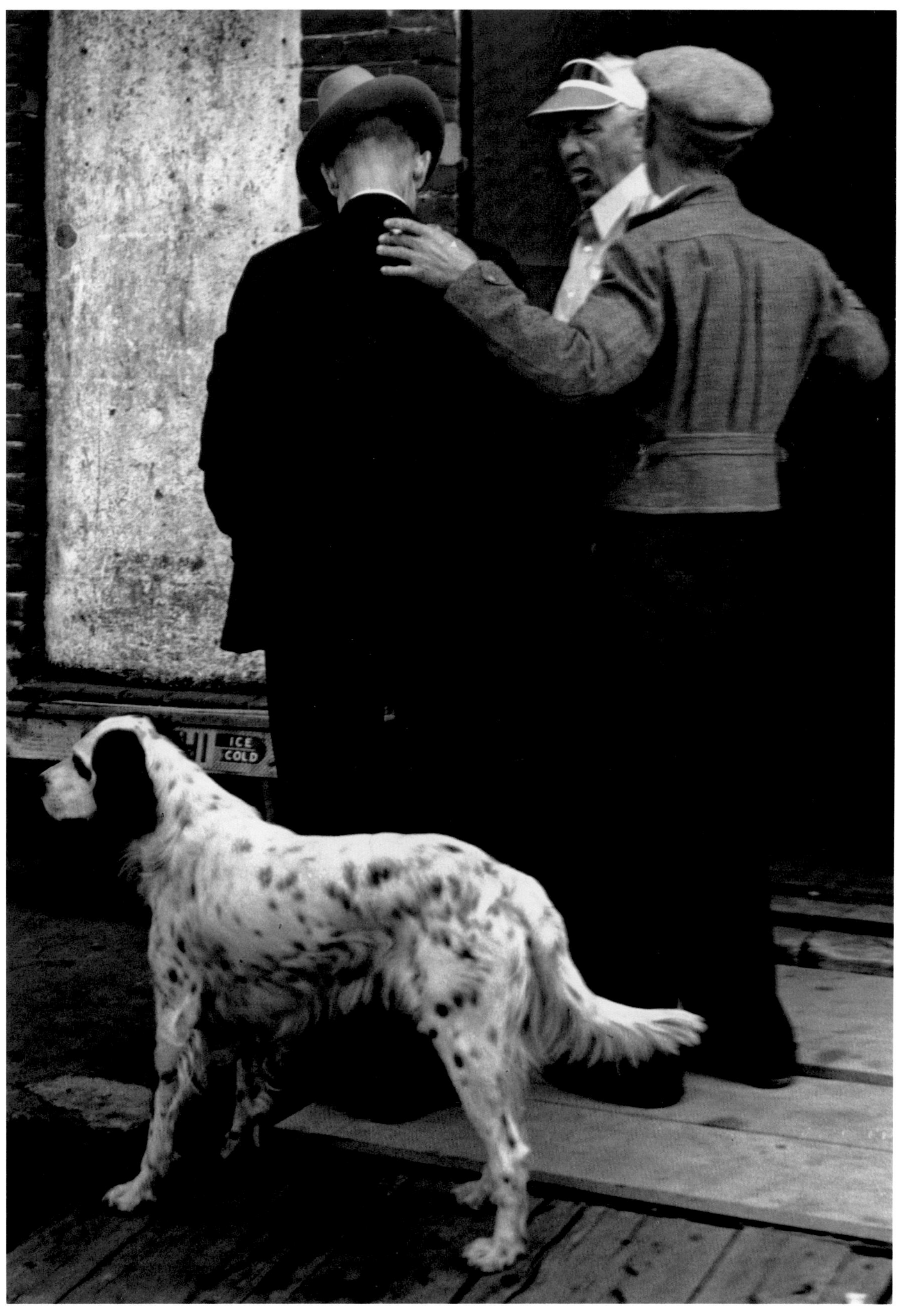

Plate 16 (cat. no. 39). *Hornitos Group, Men and Dog,* about 1935.

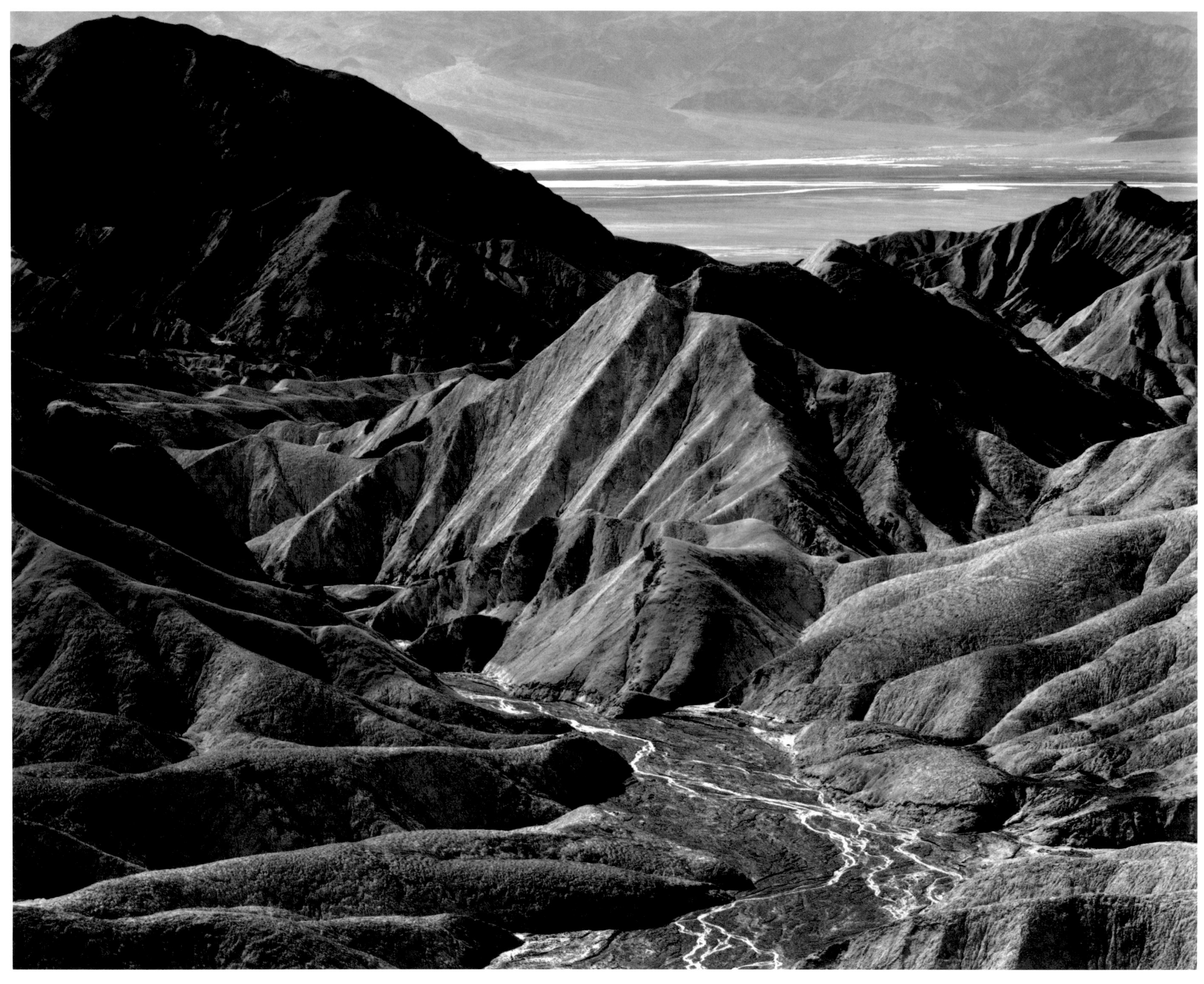

Plate 17 (cat. no. 41). *From Zabriskie Point, Death Valley National Monument,* negative about 1935, print about 1940.

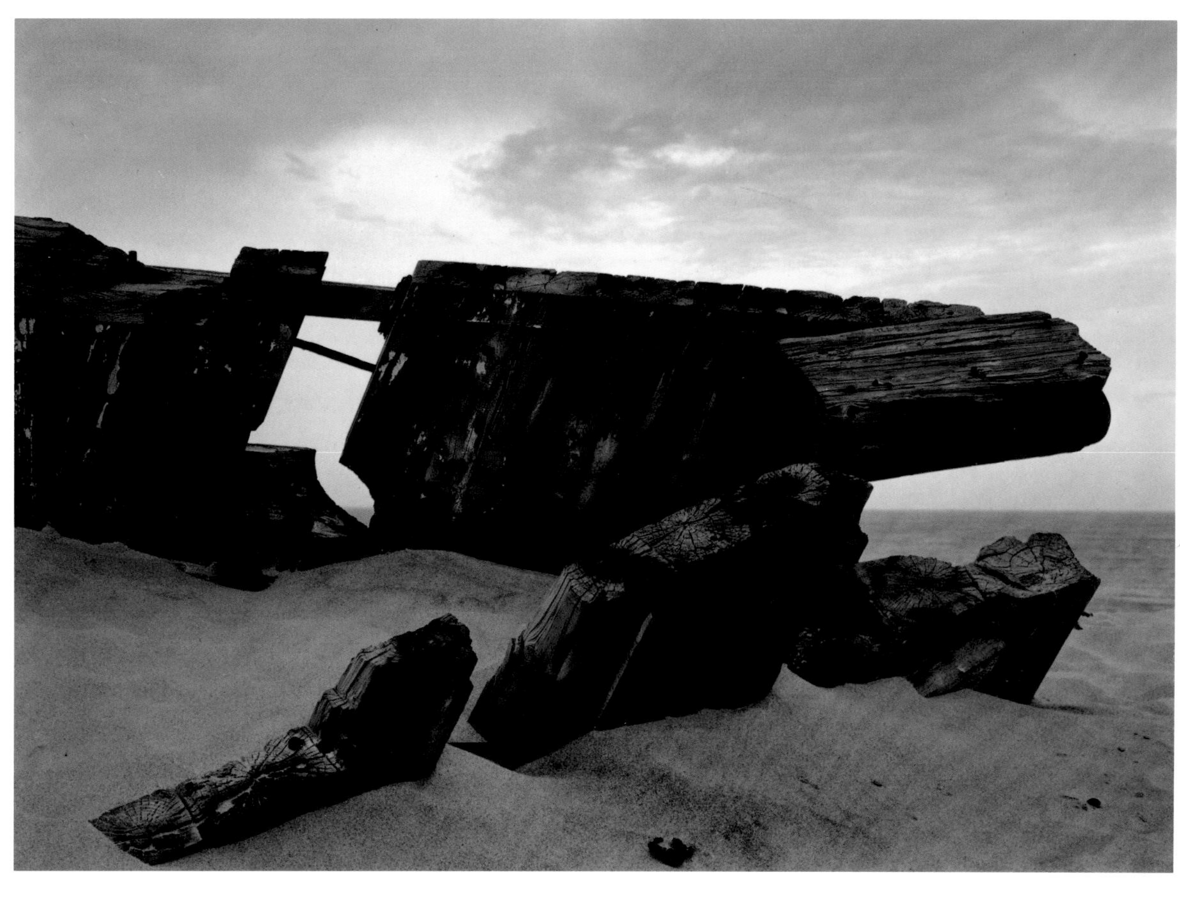

Plate 18 (cat. no. 45). *Old Wreck, Cape Cod, Massachusetts*, about 1936.

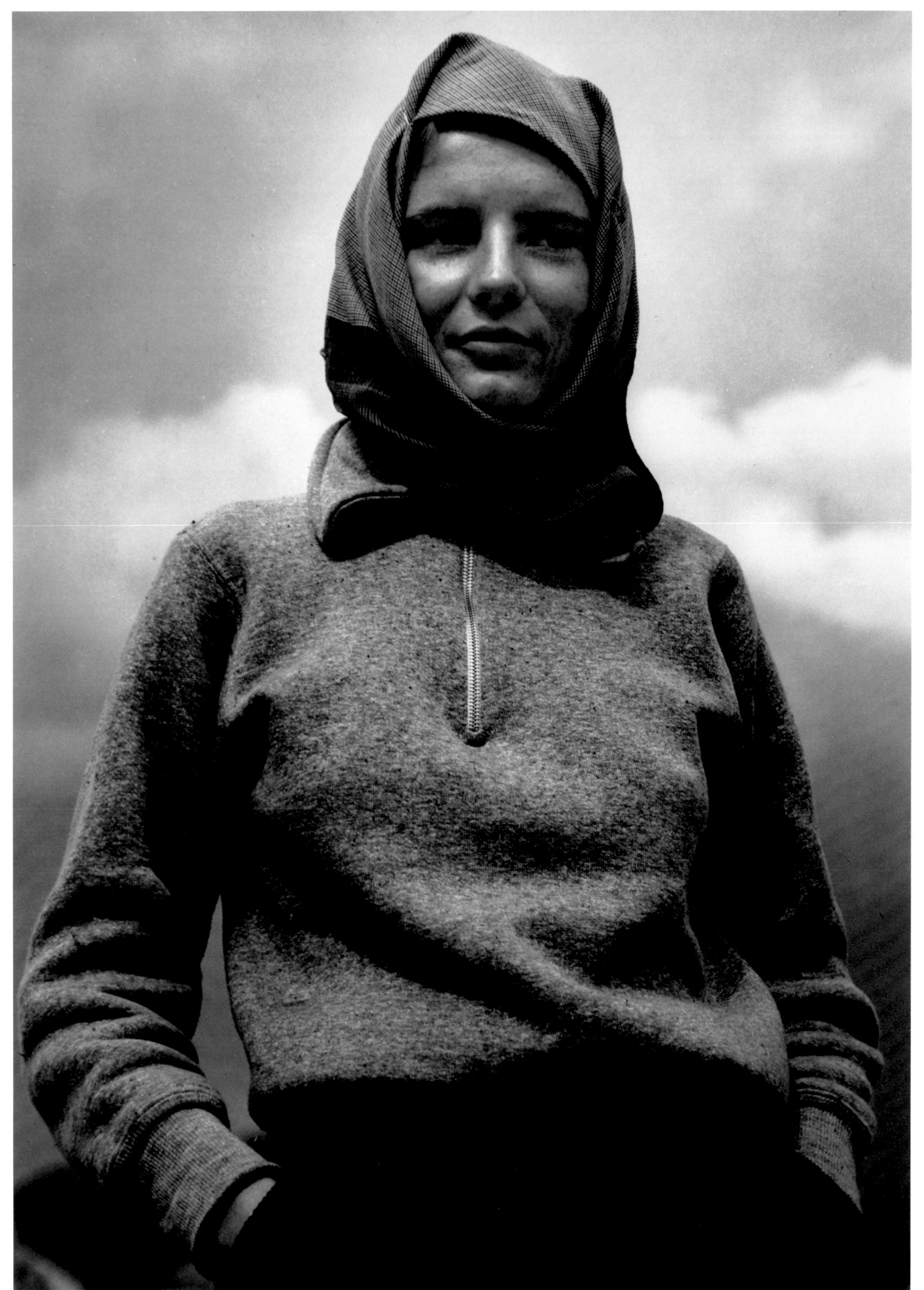

Plate 19 (cat. no. 51). *Charis Weston*, 1937.

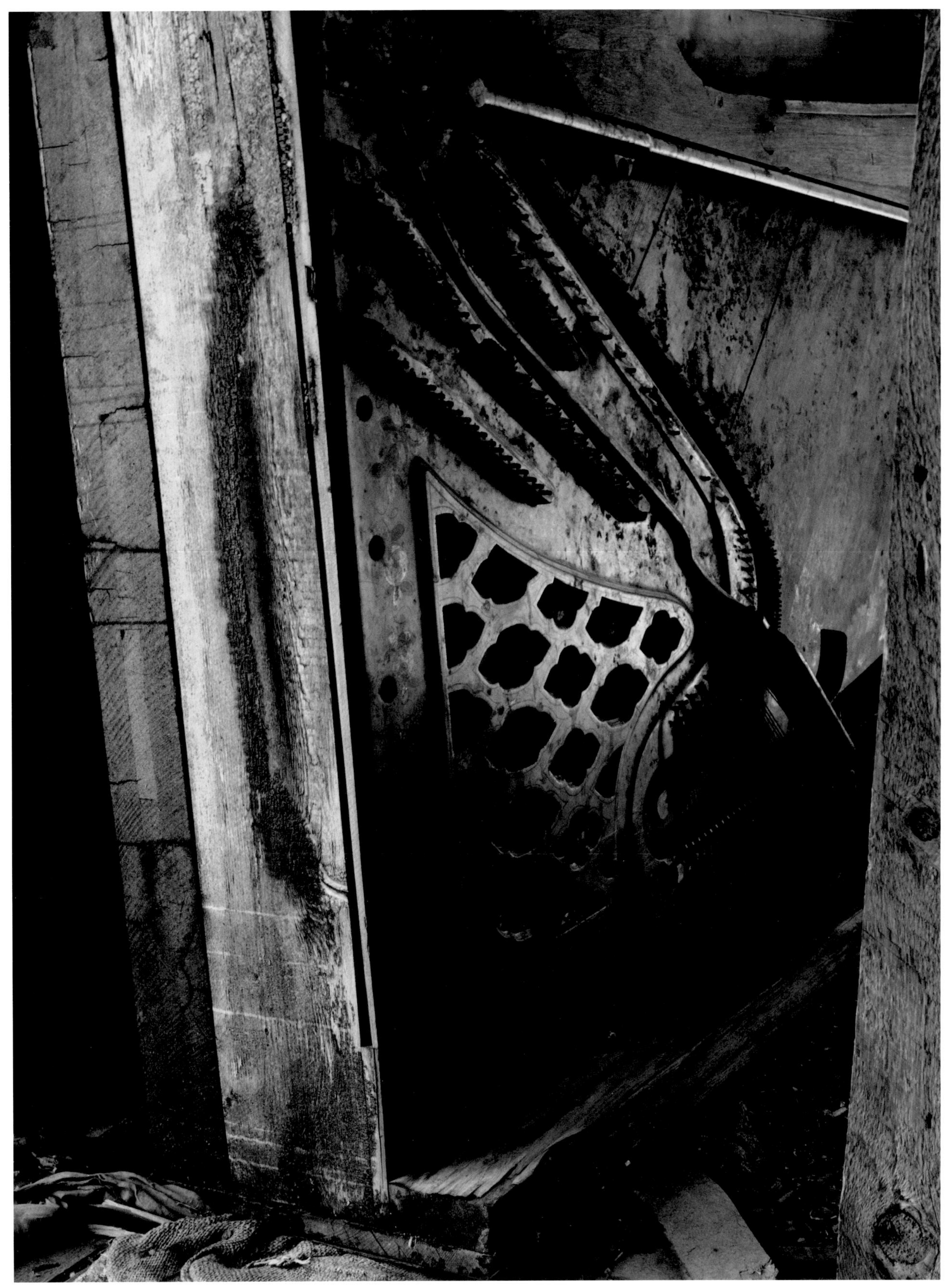

Plate 20 (cat. no. 58). *Remains of Old Square Piano, Lundy,* 1939.

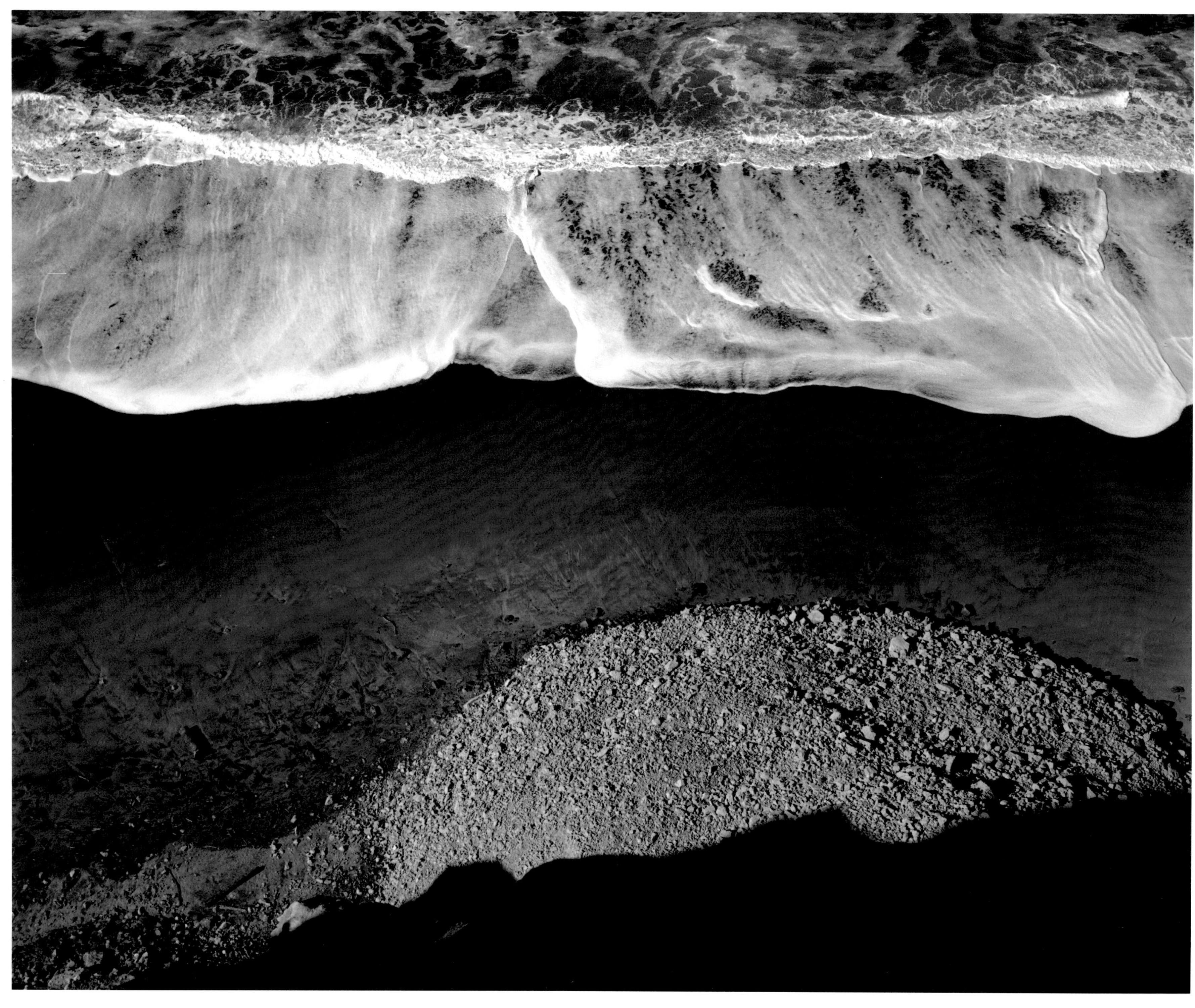

Plate 21 (cat. no. 64). *Surf Sequence #4,* negative about 1940, print about 1973.

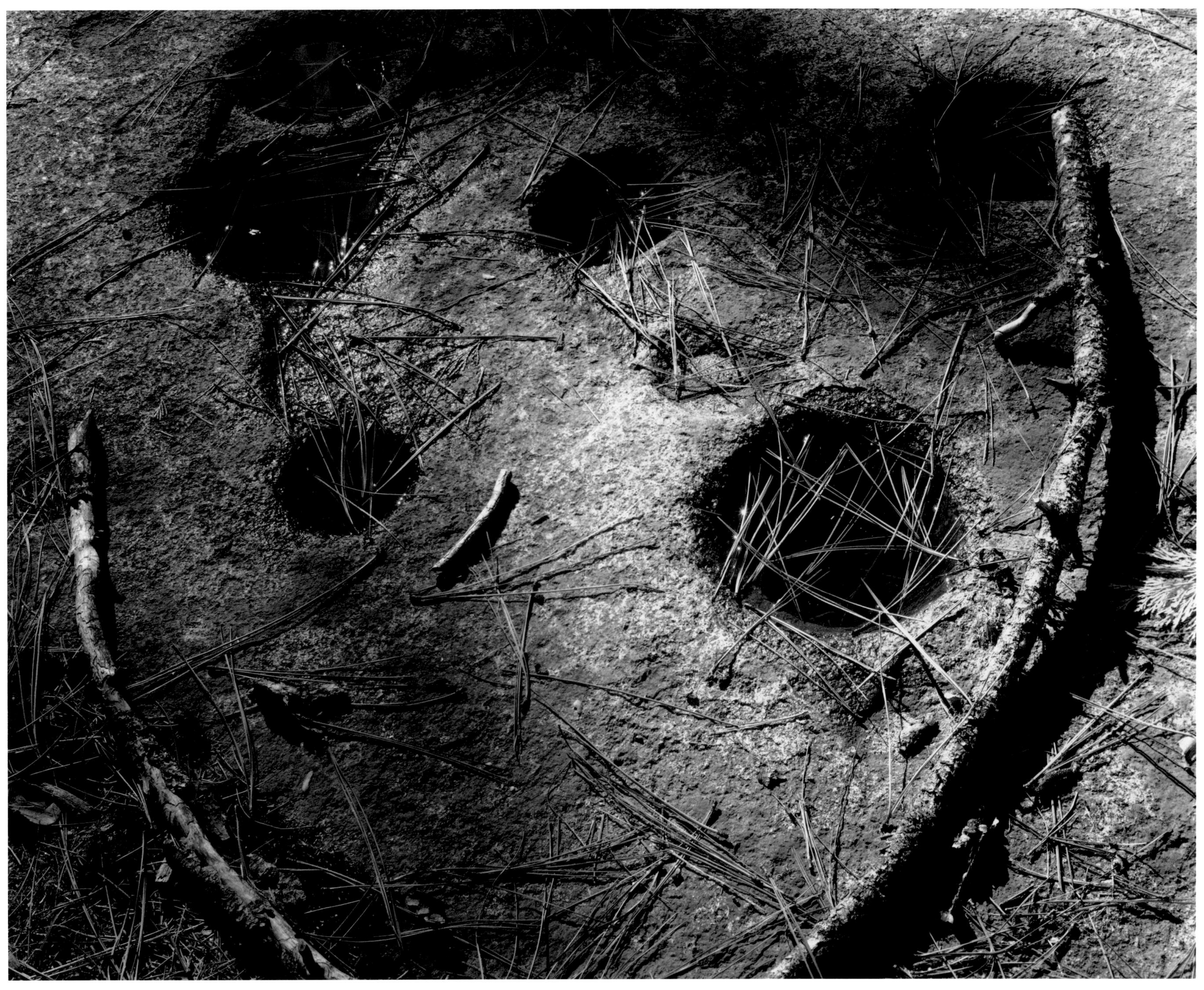

Plate 22 (cat. no. 66). *Indian Pot Holes, Big Meadow, Yosemite National Park,* about 1940.

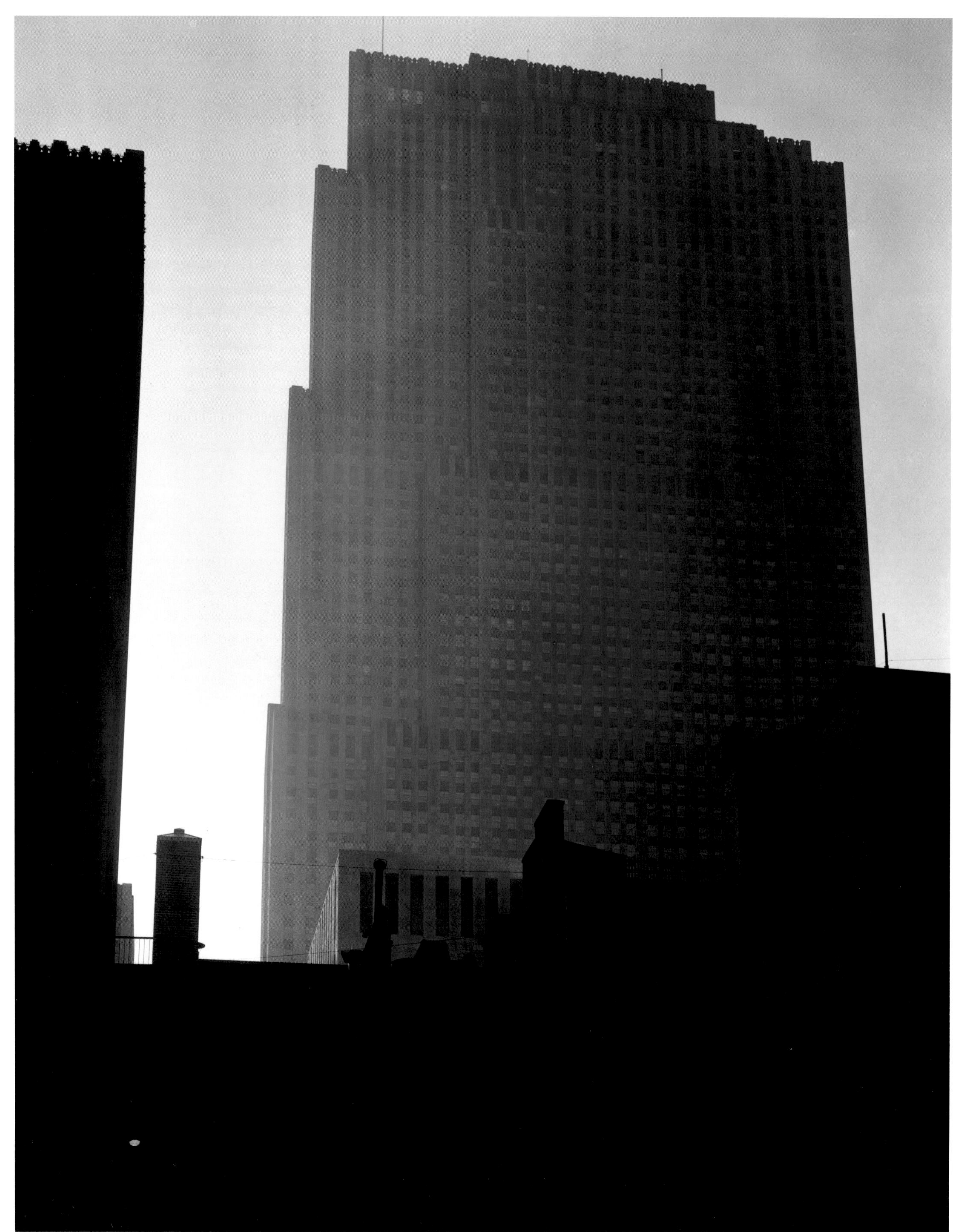

Plate 23 (cat. no. 67). *R.C.A. Building, New York,* about 1940.

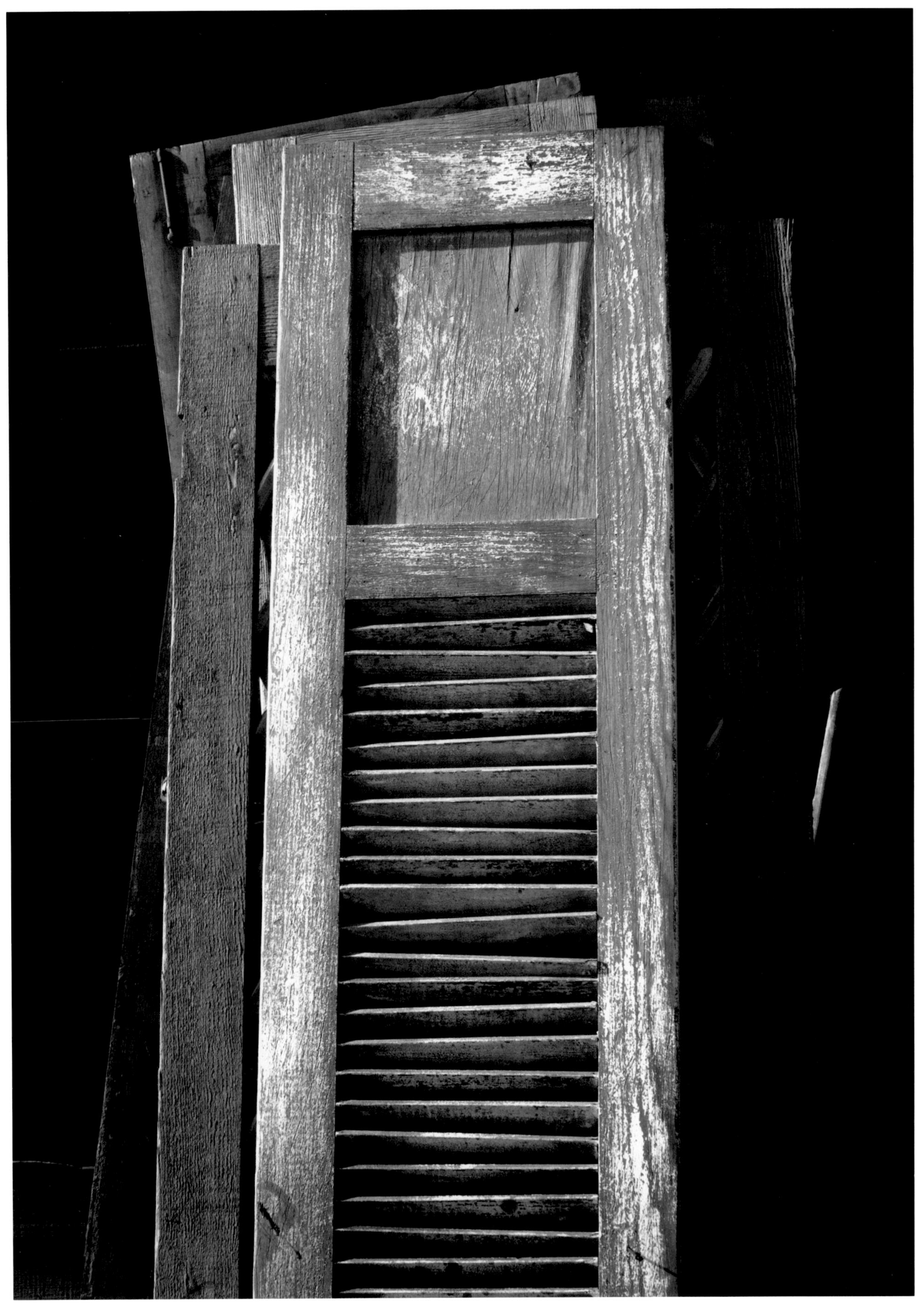

Plate 24 (cat. no. 68). *Shutters and Doors, Movie Lot,* about 1940.

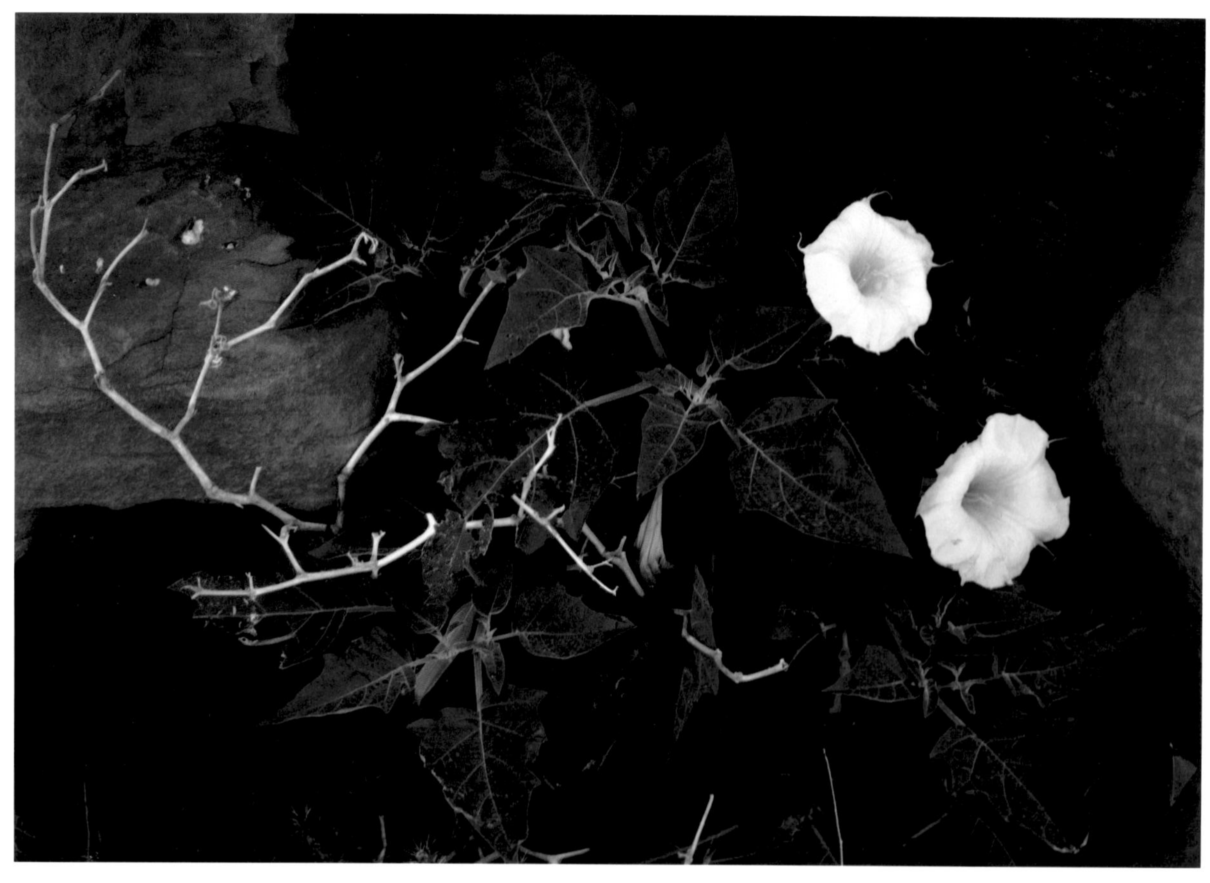

Plate 25 (cat. no. 75). *Flowers at Dusk, Canyon de Chelly National Monument,* about 1942.

CATALOGUE OF THE EXHIBITION

ANSEL ADAMS: THE EARLY YEARS

All photographs are signed on the mount, below print, right, and inscriptions are on the verso of the mount, center, and are in Adams's hand unless otherwise indicated.

All dates are in Adams's hand from the verso of the mount.

1. *"Wind,"* about 1919 (pl.1)
   Platinum print
   5 15/16" x 7 15/16"
   Signed in graphite: *Ansel E. Adams.*
   Inscribed: *"Wind,"* on mount, below print, left; *"Wind"/ Juniper Tree, Yosemite Nat Park Calif/ (very early 1919?)/Dassonville Paper;* in black ink, on verso of mount, center, Partial label *(Ansel) EASTON ADAMS/(Par)MELIAN PRINT/No. P. 79,* on verso of mount, upper left.
2. *Banner Peak — Thousand Island Lake*
   (from "Parmelian Prints of the High Sierras," 1927)
   Platinum print
   6" x 8"
   Signed in graphite: *A. E. Adams.*
   Title printed in capitals, below print, center.
3. *Glacier Point* (pl. 2)
   (from "Parmelian Prints of the High Sierras," 1927)
   Platinum print
   6" x 8"
   Signed in graphite: *A. E. Adams.*
   Title printed in capitals, below print, center.
4. *Mt. Clark*
   (from "Parmelian Prints of the High Sierras," 1927)
   Platinum print
   8" x 6"
   Signed in graphite: *A. E. Adams.*
   Title printed in capitals, below print, center.
5. *Abode of Snow*
   (from "Parmelian Prints of the High Sierras," 1927)
   Platinum print
   6" x 8"
   Signed in graphite: *A. E. Adams.*
   Title printed in capitals, below print, center.
6. *The Sentinel*
   (from "Parmelian Prints of the High Sierras," 1927)
   Platinum print
   6" x 8"
   Signed in graphite: *A. E. Adams.*
   Title printed in capitals, below print, center.
7. *Monolith — The Face of Half Dome* (pl. 6)
   (from "Parmelian Prints of the High Sierras," 1927)
   Platinum print
   8" x 6"
   Signed in graphite: *Adams.*
   Title printed in capitals, below print, center.
8. *Monolith — The Face of Half Dome* (pl. 7)
   Negative 1927, print 1950-60
   Silver print
   18 3/4" x 14 1/2"
   Signed in graphite: *Ansel Adams.*
   Inscribed verso, in black ink: *Monolith, The Face of Half Dome/ Yosemite Valley/CA 1923* [sic] *6^2 x 8^2/glass plate From the "Diving Board"/ West shoulder of Half Dome/wide-angle lens.*
9. *From Moose Pass,* 1928 (pl. 4)
   Platinum print
   6" x 8"
   Signed in graphite: *Ansel E. Adams.*
   Inscribed verso, in black ink: *From Moose Pass (Telephotograph) Canada 1928.*
10. *Mount Robson from Mount Resplendent,* 1928
    Platinum print
    8" x 6"
    Signed in graphite: *Ansel E. Adams.*
    Inscribed verso, in black ink: *Valuable only extant Print/Mount Robson From Mount Resplendent, Canada 1928/4 x 5 view camera/Dassonville Paper.*
11. *Eagle Dance,* about 1928-9 (pl. 3)
    Platinum print
    5 5/8" x 7 3/4"
    Signed in graphite: *Ansel E. Adams.*
    Inscribed verso, in black ink: *Eagle Dance/San Ildefonso Pueblo N M / 4 x 5 Original Print/Dassonville Paper.*
12. *From near Mt. Watkins, Winter, Yosemite National Park,* neg. 1929, print 1930-1932 (pl. 5)
    Silver print
    3 3/16" 4 5/8"
    Signed in graphite: *Ansel Adams.*
    Inscribed verso, in black ink: *From near Mt. Watkins Winter/Yosemite Nat. Park/1929 CA/Printed 1930 to 1932.*
13. *Interior — Penitente Morada, Northern New Mexico,* about 1930
    Silver print
    11 3/16" x 8 9/16"
    Signed in graphite: *Ansel Adams.*
    Inscribed verso, in black ink: *Interior — Penitente Morada, Norther (n) New Mexico/CA 1930.*

14. *North Palisade, Sierra Nevada,* about 1930
Silver print
9 3/8" x 6 3/4"
Signed in black ink: Ansel Adams.
Inscribed verso, in black ink: *North Palisade/Sierra Nevada/CA 1930.*

15. *Black Giant, Muir Pass, Sierra Nevada*, about 1930
Silver print
7 3/8" x 9 1/8"
Signed in black ink: *Ansel Adams.*
Inscribed verso, in black ink: *Black Giant, Muir Pass. Sierra Nevada/*[crossed out] *Black Mountain Pass. CA 1930.*

16. *Snow on Trees, Yosemite Valley,* about 1930 (pl. 8)
Silver print
8 3/16" x 5 5/8"
Signed in graphite: *Ansel Adams.*
Inscribed verso, in black ink: *Snow on Trees Yosemite Valley/ 4 x 5 Novodrom paper/1930?.*

17. *Rocks, Baker's Beach, San Francisco,* about 1931 (pl. 9)
Silver print
6 9/16" x 8 3/4"
Signed in graphite: *Ansel Adams.*
Inscribed verso in black ink: *Rocks Bakers Beach/San Francisco/ CA 1931/9 x 12 cm Original Print.*

18. *Cross, San Rafael, California,* 1932 (pl. 10)
Silver print
5 3/8" x 6 5/8"
Signed in black ink: *Ansel Adams.*
Inscribed verso, in black ink: *Cross. San Rafael Calif/California/ 1932/4 x 5 view camera/Protar lens.*

19. *Rose and Driftwood*
Negative 1932, print about 1963
Silver print
7 5/8" x 9 1/2"
Signed in black ink: *Ansel Adams.*
Inscribed verso, in black ink: *Rose and Driftwood San Francisco 1932/4 x 5 Camera/1963 + Print.*

20. *Adobe Church, New Mexico,* about 1932
Silver print
6 5/16" x 8 3/4"
Signed in graphite: Ansel Adams.
Inscribed verso, in black ink: *Adobe Church, New Mexico/Hernandes — Facade/ 1932 CA.*

21. *Sutro Gardens, Land's End — San Francisco*, about 1932
Silver print
13 3/4" x 10 3/8"
Signed in graphite: *Ansel Adams.*
Inscribed verso, in black ink: *Sutro's GARDEN, LAND'S end — San Francisco/CA 1932/4 x 5.*

22. *Anchors, San Francisco, California,* about 1932
Silver print
6 9/16" x 8 3/4"
Signed in graphite: *Ansel Adams.*
Inscribed verso, in black ink: *Anchors, San Francisco California/ CA 1932 Pan. Film + #29 filter/8 x 10 Original Print.*

23. *Shipwreck Series #1, Steel and Stone,* about 1932 (pl. 11)
Silver print
8 1/16" x 5 7/8"
Signed in graphite: *Ansel Adams.*
Inscribed verso, in black ink: *Shipwreck Series #1/Steel and Stone/ San Francisco/CA 1932/4 x 5 Original Print.*

24. *Shipwreck Series*
Negative about 1932, print about 1973
Silver print
7 1/4" x 9 1/2"
Signed in graphite: *Ansel Adams.*

25. *Shipwreck Series* (pl. 12)
Negative about 1932, print about 1973
Silver print
7 5/16" x 9 1/4"
Signed in graphite: *Ansel Adams.*

26. *Shipwreck Series*
Negative about 1932, print about 1973
Silver print
6 15/16" x 9 1/2"
Signed in graphite: *Ansel Adams.*

27. *Shipwreck Series*
Negative about 1932, print about 1973
Silver print
7 3/8" x 8 11/16"
Signed in graphite: *Ansel Adams.*

28. *Shipwreck Series*
Negative about 1932, print about 1973
Silver print
7 1/2" x 9 5/16"
Signed in graphite: *Ansel Adams.*

29. *"Minerva" from Sutro Gardens, San Francisco,* 1933 (pl. 13)
Silver print
9 5/16" x 6 1/2"
Signed in graphite: *Ansel E. Adams.*
Inscribed on mount, below print, left, in graphite: *From Sutro Gardens*; on verso of mount, upper left, in graphite: *Group f/64*; on verso of mount, center, in black ink: *"Minerva"/FROM SUTRO GARDE* [sic] *SF 1933.*

30. *The Golden Gate, San Francisco,* 1933
Silver print
6 9/16" x 9"

Signed in graphite: *Ansel Adams.*
Inscribed verso, in black ink: *Early Photograph/The Golden Gate 1933/ San Francisco/before the building of the Bridge/8 x 10 view camera.*

31. *Self-Portrait in Victorian Mirror,* about 1933
Silver print
13 3/8" x 9 7/8"
Signed in black ink: *Ansel Adams.*
Inscribed verso, in black ink: *Self-Portrait in Victorian Mirror/ Old Silas Palmer Home/Menlo Park, Calif/1933 CA/ 4 x 5 Camera/ Protar Lens.*

32. *Boards and Thistles,* about 1933
Silver print
9 1/8" x 6 3/4"
Signed in graphite: *Ansel Adams.*
Inscribed verso, in black ink: *Board* [sic] + *Thistles/San Francisco* [in red ink]/*CA 1933.*

33. *Mexican Section, Palm Springs, California* (pl.14)
Negative about 1934, print about 1935
Silver print
6 11/16" x 8 1/2"
Signed in graphite: *Ansel Adams.*
Inscribed verso, in black ink: *Mexican Section, Palm Springs Calif/ 1934 CA/4 x 5 Camera Print, about 1935+.*

34. *Hornitos Homecoming,* 1935
Silver print
6 1/8" x 7 5/8"
Signed in black ink: *Ansel Adams.*
Inscribed verso, in black ink: *Hornitas* [sic] *Homecoming/Detail/ Hornitas* [sic] *California/1935/Contax Photograph Original Print/ 35 mm.*

35. *Museum Storeroom*, 1935
Silver print
7" x 9 1/16"
Signed in graphite: *Ansel Adams.*
Title and date typed on Adams's label.
Inscribed verso, in black ink: *"Found" Subject/8 x 10 Camera.*

36. *Glacier Polish, Lyell Fork of the Merced River,* about 1935
Silver print
7" x 9 1/8"
Signed in black ink: Ansel Adams.
Inscribed verso, in black ink: *Glacier Polish. Lyell Fork of the Merced River/CA 1935.*

37. *Grass and Reflections in the Lyell Fork of the Merced River,* about 1935
Silver print
7 7/16" x 9 7/16"
Signed in black ink: *Ansel Adams.*
Inscribed verso, in black ink: *Grass and Reflections/In the Lyell Fork of the Merced River/Y.N.P./CA 1935.*

38. *Discussion in Art,* about 1935 (pl. 15)
Silver print
7" x 9 1/16"
Signed in graphite: *Ansel Adams.*
Inscribed verso, in blue ink: *Discussion in art/*[signed] *Ansel Adams/ANSEL ADAMS/Not for Sale/CA 1935/Contax Photograph.*

39. *Hornitos Group, Men and Dog,* about 1935 (pl. 16)
Silver print
8 11/16" x 6 1/8"
Signed in graphite: *Ansel Adams.*
Title typed on Adams's label.
Inscribed verso, in black ink: *CA 1935/Original Print/Contax 35mm.*

40. *Residents, Hornitos, California,* about 1935
Silver print
13 13/16" x 10 5/8"
Signed in graphite: *Ansel Adams.*
Inscribed verso, in black ink: *Residents/Hornitos, Calif/ Original Print (early)/"Old Timers"/CA 1935.*

41. *From Zabriskie Point, Death Valley National Monument* (pl.17)
Negative about 1935, print about 1940
Silver print
7 5/8" x 9 5/8"
Signed in graphite: *Ansel Adams.*
Inscribed verso, in blue ink: *From Zabriskie Point/Death Valley National Monument/California Ansel Adams/* [in black ink] *1935/ca/ 8 x 10/camera/Print about 1940.*

42. *Burned Trees, Owens Valley, California,* about 1936
Silver print
13 1/8" x 9 3/16"
Signed in black ink: *Ansel Adams.*
Inscribed verso, in black ink: *Burned Trees. Owens Valley, Calif/ CA 1936.*

43. *Oak Trees, Winter, Yosemite Valley,* about 1936
Silver print
7 1/2" x 9 3/8"
Signed in graphite: *Ansel Adams.*
Inscribed verso, in black ink: *Winter, Yosemite Valley/Oak Trees. Winter. Yosemite Valley/CA 1936.*

44. *Winter, Yosemite Valley,* about 1936
Silver print
9 3/16" x 12 15/16"
Signed in graphite: *Ansel Adams.*
Inscribed verso, in black ink: *Winter, Yosemite Valley/ CA 1936.*

45. *Old Wreck, Cape Cod, Massachusetts,* about 1936 (pl. 18)
Silver print
4 1/2" x 6 1/4"
Signed in graphite: *Ansel Adams.*

Inscribed verso, in black ink: *OLD WRECK CAPE COD MASS. 1936 CA/ Wreck Shore/Cape Cod Massachusetts/Novobrom Paper/5 x 7 Linhoxx Camera/Protar lens.*

46. *Westport, California,* about 1936
Silver print
11 3/4" x 15 11/16"
Signed in graphite: *Ansel Adams.*
Inscribed verso, in black ink: *West Port* (sic), *California/CA 1936/ 8 x 10.*

47. *Grass and Burned Stump,* about 1936
Silver print
11 3/16" x 7 7/8"
Signed in black ink: *Ansel Adams.*
Inscribed verso, in black ink: *Grass and Burned Stump CA 1936/ 4 x 5.*

48. *Grass and Burned Stump*
Negative about 1936, print 1950-60
Silver print
18 5/8" x 11 9/16"
Inscribed verso, in black ink: *Grass and Burned Stump.*

49. *Winter, Yosemite Valley — Oaks in Mist*
Negative 1936-8, print 1963
Silver print
7 5/8" x 9 3/8"
Signed in black ink: *Ansel Adams.*
Inscribed verso, in black ink: *Winter. Yosemite Valley — Oaks in Mist/8 x 10 camera/1963 print.*

50. *Edward Weston, Lake Tenaya, Yosemite National Park,* 1937
Silver print
9 1/2" x 7 9/16"
Signed in graphite: *Ansel Adams.*
Inscribed verso, in black ink: *EDWARD WESTON, LAKE TENAYA, YOSEMITE NATIONAL PARK, 1937/8 x 10 Camera.*

51. *Charis Weston,* 1937 (pl. 19)
Silver print
9 1/2" x 6 13/16"
Signed in graphite: *Ansel Adams.*
Inscribed verso, in black ink: *Charis Weston/*[signed]*Ansel Adams/ CA 1938.*

52. *Political Sign,* 1937
Silver print
9 1/2" x 7 3/8"
Signed in graphite: *Ansel Adams.*
Typed on Adams's label: *TEXTURE,* and crossed out.
Inscribed verso, in black ink: *Political Sign — 1937/8 x 10 Original Print.*

53. *Thunderstorm, New Mexico*
Negative 1937, print about 1948
Silver print
6 1/2" x 9"
Signed in graphite: *Ansel Adams.*
Inscribed verso, in black ink: *Thunderstorm, New Mexico 1937/ Ghost Ranch/Print about 1948/5 x 7 Camera.*

54. *Stove in Pennsylvania Farmyard,* 1938
Silver print
9 9/16" x 12 1/2"
Signed in graphite: *Ansel Adams.*
Title and date typed on Adams's label

55. *Rear of Church — Cordova, New Mexico,* about 1938
Silver print
9 11/16" x 12 7/16"
Signed in black ink: *Ansel Adams.*
Inscribed verso, in black ink: *Rear of Church — CORDOVA, N Mex CA 1938/8 x 10 camera.*

56. *Lake Tahoe Thunderstorm*, about 1938
Silver print
13" x 10 1/2"
Signed in graphite: *Ansel Adams.*
Inscribed verso, in black ink: *LAKE TAHOE. THUNDERSTORM./CA 1938.*

57. *Old Wall Paper in House at Lundy, California,* 1939
Silver print
12 3/4" x 9"
Signed in graphite: *Ansel Adams.*
Title and date typed on Adams's label.

58. *Remains of Old Square Piano, Lundy,* 1939 (pl. 20)
Silver print
8 7/8" x 6 11/16"
Signed in graphite: *Ansel Adams.*
Title and date typed on Adams's label.
Inscribed verso, in black ink: *4 x 5 camera/original not toned.*

59. *Cemetery, New Jersey*, 1939
Silver print
9" x 7"
Signed in graphite: *Ansel Adams.*
Inscribed verso, in black ink: *Cemetery, New Jersey 1939/4 x 5 Original Print.*

60. *Mt. Williamson, Sierra Nevada, from Manzanar,* about 1939-40
Silver print
6 1/2" x 9 3/8"
Signed in graphite: *Ansel Adams.*
Inscribed verso, in black ink: *Mt. Williamson CA 1939-40/ Sierra Nevada/From Manzanar/*(signed) *Ansel Adams/ negative damaged/ Ansar "Flemish Gold" Toner/"Selenium"/split-tone 8 x 10 View Camera.*

61. *Surf Sequence #1*
Negative about 1940, print about 1973
Silver print
10 3/8" x 12 11/16"
Signed in graphite: *Ansel Adams.*

62. *Surf Sequence #2*
Negative about 1940, print about 1973
Silver print
10 1/4" x 12 11/16"
Signed in graphite: *Ansel Adams.*

63. *Surf Sequence #3,*
Negative about 1940, print about 1973
Silver print
10 3/8" x 12 11/16"
Signed in graphite: *Ansel Adams.*

64. *Surf Sequence #4,* (pl. 21)
Negative about 1940, print about 1973
Silver print
10 5/8" x 12 11/16"
Signed in graphite: *Ansel Adams.*

65. *Surf Sequence #5,*
Negative about 1940, print about 1973
Silver print
10 7/16" x 12 11/16"
Signed in graphite: *Ansel Adams.*

66. *Indian Pot Holes, Big Meadow, Yosemite National Park,* about 1940 (pl. 22)
Silver print
7 1/2" x 9 5/16"
Signed in graphite: *Ansel Adams.*
Inscribed verso, in black ink: *INDIAN POT HOLES BIG MEADOW, / Yosemite National Park/CA 1940/8 x 10.*

67. *R.C.A. Building, New York,* about 1940 (pl. 23)
Silver print
13 1/8" x 10 7/16"
Signed in black ink: *Ansel Adams.*
Inscribed verso, in black ink: *R.C.A. Bld./New York City/1940/CA.*

68. *Shutters and Doors, Movie Lot,* about 1940 (pl. 24)
Silver print
9 5/16" x 6 3/4"
Signed in graphite: *Ansel Adams.*
Inscribed verso, in red ink: *Shutters and Doors./Movie Lot./* [black ink] *Original Print/CA 1940.*

69. *Moonrise, Hernandez, New Mexico*
Negative 1941, print 1950-60
Silver print
21" x 28 7/8"
Signed in black ink: *Ansel Adams.*

70. *Carlsbad Caverns, New Mexico,* about 1941
Silver print
7 5/8" x 9 7/16"
Signed in black ink: *Ansel Adams.*
Inscribed verso, in black ink: *Carlsbad Caverns New Mexico/ National Park/CA 1941.*

71. *Forest, Mount Rainier National Park,* about 1941
Silver print
9 1/2" x 7 7/16"
Signed in graphite: *Ansel Adams.*
Inscribed verso, in blue ink: *Forest, Mount Rainier National Park/Washington/8 x 10*; stamped on verso of mount, right center *from MY CAMERA IN THE NATIONAL PARKS;* inscribed right center in blue ink: *Not for Sale Separately/CA 1941.*

72. *In Joshua Tree National Monument,* about 1941
Silver print
7 9/16" x 9 3/8"
Signed in black ink: *Ansel Adams.*
Inscribed verso, in blue ink: *IN JOSHUA Tree NAT'L MONUMENT (CALIF) PRINT #9 USED IN PORTFOLIO II/CIRCA 1941.*

73. *Old Faithful Geyser, Yellowstone National Park, Wyoming,* about 1941
Silver print
12 5/8" x 9"
Signed in graphite: *Ansel Adams.*
Inscribed verso, in black ink: *Old Faithful Geyser/Yellowstone National Park Wyoming/1941 CA/Original Print.*

74. *Long Beach Cemetery*, about 1941
Silver print
9 15/16" x 12"
Signed in black ink: *Ansel Adams.*
Inscribed verso, in black ink: *Long Beach Cemetery/ CA 1941.*

75. *Flowers at Dusk, Canyon de Chelly National Monument,* about 1942 (pl. 25)
Silver print
4 1/2" x 6 7/16"
Signed in graphite: *Ansel Adams.*
Inscribed verso, in red ink: *Flowers as Dusk/Canyon de Chelle* [sic] *Nat Monument/Arizona/CA 1942.*

SELECTED BIBLIOGRAPHY

Adams, Ansel. "Creative Photography," *Art in America,* 45 (Winter 1957-8), pp. 33-37.

Adams, Ansel. *Examples The Making of 40 Photographs,* Boston, 1983.

Adams, Ansel. *Photographs of the Southwest,* Boston, 1976.

Adams, Ansel, with Mary Street Alinder. *Ansel Adams an Autobiography,* Boston, 1985.

Alinder, James, ed. Ansel Adams 1902-1984 Untitled 37, Carmel, California, 1984.

Alinder, James and Nicolai Cikovsky, Jr. *Ansel Adams: Classic Images* The Museum Set, Boston, 1985.

Alinder, Mary Street and Andrea Gray Stillman, eds. *Ansel Adams Letters and Images 1916-1984,* Boston, 1984.

Brooks, Paul, intro. *Ansel Adams Yosemite and the Range of Light,* Boston, 1979.

Gray, Andrea. *Ansel Adams An American Place, 1936,* Tucson, 1982.

Newhall, Nancy. *Ansel Adams Volume I The Eloquent Light,* San Francisco, 1963.

Robertson, David. *West of Eden A History of the Art and Literature of Yosemite,* Yosemite, 1984.

Szarkowski, John, ed. *The Portfolios of Ansel Adams,* Boston, 1977.

ACKNOWLEDGMENTS

This exhibition has been made possible by the great generosity and kindness of Mr. and Mrs. William H. Lane. All of the photographs in the exhibition have been lent from the Lane Collection and William H. Lane also generously shared with us his personal correspondence with Ansel Adams.

This exhibition has been jointly organized by the Department of Paintings and the Department of Prints, Drawings and Photographs at the Museum of Fine Arts. We are deeply indebted to Clifford S. Ackley, curator of prints, drawings, and photographs, and Anne E. Havinga, curatorial assistant, for their expertise and their involvement in this project.

Virginia Adams deserves special thanks for sharing her insight into her husband's work, and Charis Wilson provided us with her personal view of Adams. Carl Zahn, director of publications at the Museum of Fine Arts, has collaborated on this exhibition, assisting in the selection of the photographs and bringing his great abilities to the design and production of this volume. Richard M. A. Benson is responsible for the quality of the reproduction of the prints and Cynthia Purvis has expertly edited the text. We are also grateful to Gail English, exhibitions preparator, Department of prints, drawings, and photographs for the framing of the photographs, and to Andrew Haines, conservation assistant, Paintings Department, for his assistance. Also in the Paintings Department, Erica Hirshler, assistant curator, helped in the early planning and Harriet Rome Pemstein diligently prepared the manuscript and, along with Janet Comey, provided us with much needed help. We are also grateful to Patricia Loiko, associate registrar and Désirée Caldwell, Assistant Director, Exhibitions. Finally, we thank Alan Shestack, Director of the Museum, for his enthusiastic support of this exhibition.

We also express our heartfelt thanks to Susan C. Ricci, Michael, Zoë, and Molly Quinn, Norma and Joseph Quinn, and Ellen and Paul Funk for their support.

K.E.Q. T.E.S., Jr.